FLORIDA 4-H
A CENTURY OF YOUTH SUCCESS

BY JULIE S. WILSON AND LAURA C. LOK

THE
DONNING COMPANY
PUBLISHERS

FLORIDA 4-H

A CENTURY OF YOUTH SUCCESS

MANATEE COUNTY 4-H CLUBS WELCOME YOU

The Donning Company Publishers
184 Business Park Drive, Suite 206
Virginia Beach, VA 23462

Steve Mull, General Manager
Barbara Buchanan, Office Manager
Heather Floyd, Editor
Jennifer Peñaflor, Graphic Designer
Derek Eley, Imaging Artist
Lori Kennedy, Project Research Coordinator
Scott Rule, Director of Marketing
Tonya Hannink, Marketing Coordinator

Bernie Walton, Project Director

Library of Congress Cataloging-in-Publication Data

Wilson, Julie S., 1981-
  Florida 4-H : a century of youth success / by Julie S. Wilson and Laura C. Lok.
      p. cm.
  Includes bibliographical references.
  ISBN 978-1-57864-518-3 (hardcover : alk. paper)
  1. 4-H clubs--Florida--History. I. Lok, Laura C., 1975- II. Title.
  S533.F66W55 2008
  630.71'709759--dc22
                            2008024904

Printed in the United States of America at Walsworth Publishing Company

TABLE OF CONTENTS

(table of contents continued on next page)

ACKNOWLEDGMENTS

The authors recognize that this book would not have been possible without the invaluable assistance of many people, including Extension agents, 4-H volunteers, and state staff. Thank you to all of those that have provided photographs and information for this book. Thanks to Bernie Walton and Heather Floyd of The Donning Company Publishers for your help and patience during this whole process. We would like to recognize and thank the Florida 4-H Foundation, Inc., for their financial support for this book. Thank you to all who support the Florida 4-H Youth Development Program.

PREFACE

We are excited to celebrate the 100th Anniversary of 4-H in Florida. It was 1909 when J. J. Vernon, dean of the College of Agriculture at the University of Florida, first organized corn clubs for boys in Alachua, Bradford, and Marion counties. Similarly, programs for girls were organized beginning in 1912. The girls' clubs were named tomato clubs. From these clubs, the Florida 4-H program was born.

From the very beginning, the focus of the 4-H program has been youth development. The projects and methods of reaching youth have changed continuously, but the dedication to assist youth in building lasting relationships and developing life skills for the past one hundred years has been our steadfast commitment. We are proud that 4-H is reaching over 225,000 youth annually with positive youth experiences.

Thank you to the authors that organized this book. Thank you to the centennial committee for the organization of the entire 4-H Centennial Celebration. We believe that in celebrating our rich history, we are also committing to continuing the strong 4-H programs in Florida for the future.

DR. LARRY ARRINGTON | DEAN FOR EXTENSION | INSTITUTE OF FOOD AND AGRICULTURAL SCIENCES | UNIVERSITY OF FLORIDA

FOREWORD

Of the innumerable challenges facing American agriculture today, I can think of few more daunting than replacing today's agricultural producers. The average farmer in this country is fifty-seven years old, and unlike previous generations that were characterized by larger families and fewer opportunities outside the family farm, many children raised on farms today have no interest in following in their parents' footsteps.

It is precisely for that reason that 4-H may be even more important today than when the organization was founded one hundred years ago. If we do not expose young people in sufficient numbers to the joys and challenges of raising things in the great outdoors, we will be unable to sustain an agricultural industry in this nation. It is just that simple.

For a century now, 4-H has been producing farmers, ranchers, and agricultural professionals who have been the envy of the world. Not only have we been able to provide ample bounty for our citizens, but our products have fed—and continue to feed—people throughout the world. A roster of 4-H alumni reads like a "Who's Who" of American achievement: Roy Rogers, John Denver, Dolly Parton, Alan Shepard, Don Meredith, Charley Pride, Orville Redenbacher, and Reba McIntyre. In all, nearly fifty million Americans have participated in 4-H programs.

In the late 1950s and early '60s, I was one of them. I recall growing a vegetable garden each year and learning how to produce sweet corn, potatoes, and squash. I even earned a blue ribbon or two for my efforts. And I recall that the highlight of my summers back then was the week we spent at 4-H camp, alternating each year between Camp Cloverleaf near Sebring and Ocala National Forest Camp.

Like millions of other 4-H alumni, I've made a career in the agricultural industry thanks in large part to the dedicated teachers and volunteers who taught me many lifelong lessons that will remain with me forever.

For one hundred years now, 4-H has been a vital entry point for young people interested in farming careers. "Learning by doing" was an early motto of the organization, which was created in 1909 to improve life in rural areas. During World War II, its mission changed as it devoted its energies to victory gardens, which brought 4-H in contact with urban populations. The organization has constantly adapted to a changing world—like the professional agricultural producers it trained who have always demonstrated the flexibility to adapt to society's changing tastes and needs.

Today, its various missions remain largely intact, yet it carries an added burden of encouraging young people to explore the possibilities of a career in agriculture or in agriculture-related fields in an ever-increasingly urbanized nation. If the past is any guide, 4-H will be up to the task.

CHARLES H. BRONSON | COMMISSIONER OF AGRICULTURE | STATE OF FLORIDA

FLORIDA 4-H

A HISTORY

Contributed by: Ami Neiberger-Miller, a former member of the state 4-H staff at the University of Florida, where she managed teen leadership programs, public relations outreach, publications production, and communication arts. She holds a master's degree in history from the University of Florida and has worked with the National 4-H Council and the National 4-H Cooperative Curriculum System. In 2003, she founded Steppingstone, LLC, a company that provides public relations, design, writing, and training services.

Today's 4-H projects range from aerospace and citizenship to horses and poultry. But the first 4-H members didn't have quite as large a selection of projects to choose from. Like many other parts of the United States, 4-H work began with corn and tomato clubs.

THE EARLY DAYS
CORN AND TOMATO CLUBS

The first 4-H clubs in the Sunshine State were corn clubs for boys, organized in 1909 in Alachua, Bradford, and Marion counties by J. J. Vernon, the dean of agriculture at the University of Florida (UF).

The first County Extension agents faced many challenges—not the least of which was getting around. "The Florida County Agent was truly an agricultural missionary, riding his circuits preaching the doctrine of a better way of agriculture and a better life," wrote J. Lee Smith, District Extension agent, who worked with 4-H programs in Florida in the 1920s. "This missionary, riding a 'circuit' on horseback, on a road cart, or in a buggy, made his contacts slowly. Consequently, the corn club members for the first year, 1910, were enrolled in the fall of 1909."

Each boy was given seed corn to plant. An exhibit and report were made the following fall, with the goal of encouraging farmers to plant new varieties of seed corn. The boys were often able to grow twice as much corn on a plot as had grown previously, thereby doubling production. By growing additional corn, families were able to better

Nassau County Corn Club Contest, 1915

meet their own needs, maximize the efficiency of their farming operations, and earn more money.

In 1911, A. P. Spencer from UF's agricultural college continued the work begun with corn clubs. By 1914, 935 boys were enrolled and 308 "corn club boys" turned in records about their experiences growing corn.

Girls in the 4-H Club not only learn better home practices, they show others the methods that they use. Tomato canning demonstration, 1928.

Tomato clubs began in 1912, when Agnes Ellen Harris left her position at Florida State College for Women (FSCW, now known as Florida State University), to become Florida's first home demonstration agent. While preparing at Columbia for Extension work, she heard about the tomato clubs that were forming all over the United States and encouraging girls to grow tomatoes and can them.

She volunteered her services to start tomato clubs in Leon County, and $150 of the $200 allotted for her salary was used to hire a horse and buggy so she could travel around the county. Ironically, the person charged with starting Florida 4-H's tomato clubs had no experience in canning.

Before her first demonstration, which was held at the courthouse in Gainesville, Harris spent a frantic weekend at home practicing Braezele's canning methods. While her home experiments were well-preserved, her first demonstration alongside O. B. Martin anything but smooth. She remembered:

> The picture is still in my mind of the open trunk, the table full of cans and soldering irons, the machine, the little zinc contraption for holding fire for heating the irons, the earnestly interested

Tomato exhibit in 1912, Escambia County

> women employed as home demonstration agents, and Mr. Vernon, Mr. Martin, and a few other men connected with the University. All went well, until the time came for sealing the cans, and they would not seal, although we worked well and read directions and followed Mr. Martin's instructions. It became time for the picnic Mr. J. J. Vernon had planned, and so the group left.

Eventually, the cans were sealed that day. In spite of a rocky start, Harris's efforts soon met with great success. Within the first year, she enrolled more than 500 girls in tomato clubs in Alachua, Bradford, Clay, Columbia, Escambia, Hillsborough, Holmes, Leon, Madison, Pasco, and Walton counties.

A 4-H club tomato garden, raised by Fern and Fay Brasington. Madison County, June 27, 1940.

Home demonstration agents would visit rural schools, talk about the club, and leave enrollment cards for girls ages ten to eighteen. After getting their parents' permission to join, the girls would mail their cards to the agent. Each girl was given tomato seed, planting instructions, and a record book. The home demonstration agent soon visited to help plan how the tomatoes would be planted on a one-tenth-acre plot. Before harvest time, the agent would visit each neighborhood to demonstrate canning methods.

For many rural families, a 4-H tomato plot provided additional food for the table and earned additional income. Additionally, the canned goods placed on the shelves used up farm bounty that could not be sold or did not go to market, expanded the family diet, and provided security in a world where some families did not eat year-round.

Harris continued her Extension work for several years, even in the face of opposition from some other FSCW faculty members, who wondered why a university professor would be doing such practical work. In 1914, 373 tomato club girls canned 184,821 pounds of tomatoes. In other words, each girl canned on average nearly 500 pounds of tomatoes.

The 4-H work was further aided by Mrs. W. S. Jennings, the chairman of education for the Florida Federation of Women's Clubs, who asked county commissions to designate funds for both home demonstration and 4-H work. This melding of state, county, and private support would mirror the funding structure used by 4-H and Extension programs a hundred years later.

Club boy selling sweet potato plants, Jefferson County

13

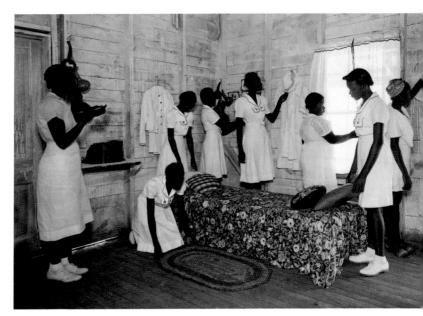

Thrift exhibit by the Negro 4-H Club of Archer. Bessie Brown was the local leader. Alachua County, June 26, 1940.

Extension work with African-Americans began in Florida in 1915 and was headquartered at Florida A&M University (FAMU). As was common in the southern United States at that time, 4-H work was segregated. About 1,250 boys and girls were enrolled in farm-makers' clubs and homemakers' clubs in 1917 in Alachua, Gadsden, Jefferson, Leon, Marion, and Washington counties. The boys cultivated a half-acre of corn, a one-fourth acre of peanuts, and a one-fourth acre of sweet potatoes. The girls grew a one-tenth acre of tomatoes and preserved many farm products.

By 1920, African-American 4-H club work had expanded to eighteen counties. The program for men and boys was expanded to include corn clubs, potato clubs, pig clubs, and savings clubs. For the girls, there were canning clubs, poultry clubs, improvement clubs, dairy clubs, sanitation clubs, and savings clubs.

"Nothing did more toward gaining sentiment in favor of the work," noted A. A. Turner, who supervised Extension work with African-Americans in Florida for twenty-nine years, when talking about the powerful impact fair exhibits had on community support and participation. Exhibits at the state and county fairs showing the work done by 4-H members were a source of pride, while demonstrations locally and at the state fair taught new agricultural techniques and developed public speaking skills for youth.

For its first fifty-four years, 4-H educational programs for Caucasian boys were administered by the state 4-H staff in Gainesville at UF, the program for Caucasian girls was overseen by staff at FSCW in Tallahassee, while separate programs for African-American boys and girls were managed through FAMU.

4-H CLUBS EXPAND
TO NEW PROJECTS, SHORT COURSES, COUNCILS, AND NATIONAL TRIPS

It was not long before 4-H interests expanded beyond corn and tomatoes. The next addition to the program was a swine project, which was offered to boys in 1916. During the first year, 652 young men enrolled in swine-raising activities.

Then came cotton, sweet potatoes, farm animals, forestry, wildlife conservation, home beautification, and nearly all phases of agriculture. The expansion of 4-H into these new areas of study for boys was overseen by R. W. Blacklock, who served as State Boys' 4-H Club agent for more than thirty-three years.

While attending canning bees, the "tomato club girls" began asking their home demonstration agents, "When are you going to teach us to sew?" So, new programs began in sewing, nutrition, food preparation, home improvement, home beautification, and most phases of home economics.

At the same time, attitudes toward youth work were changing. In the beginning, emphasis was placed on production. The goal was to help young people produce material wealth—to grow two bushels of corn where only one had grown before. As time passed, these ideals changed to an emphasis on the individual 4-H member, and his or her growth as a person. Opportunities were created for young people to develop physically, mentally, socially, and spiritually. The organization gradually became known as the 4-H club, with an emphasis on head, heart, hands, and health. The first published report and use of the term "4-H club" in an official publication produced by the University of Florida is found in the 1926 Annual Report.

In 1912, tomato club prize-winners were awarded trips to Tallahassee, where they took "short courses" at the Department of Home Economics at FSCW. Trips for outstanding girls in twelve counties were financed by county boards of education, county commissioners, and other organizations. Short courses for girls were held annually at FSCW from 1912 to 1964, except for three years during World War II, when gas rationing forced suspension of the event. In 1963, 460 girls attended the Girls' State Short Course in Tallahassee, where special emphasis was placed on junior leadership.

Girls were expected to engage in 4-H projects teaching them sewing, cooking, homemaking skills, and gardening. Evelyn Jones, vice president of the Girls' 4-H Club Council, wrote, "A 4-H girl has an opportunity, second to none, to prepare herself for the job of future wife and mother through her 4-H projects and activities.... We girls are preparing for that most important role—housewife and mother." The same report cited a statistic saying that 48 percent of new brides were teenagers and described a health education program conducted during the Girls' State Short Course in Tallahassee specifically to teach skills needed for homemaking and childcare.

The first Boys' Short Course was held at the University of Florida in September 1916, with seventy-three of the top 4-H club boys in the state attending. Before this event, a few boys had attended the Farmers' Short Course offered by the

15

Vernon Frazier of Hawthorne displays a prize-winning vine of peanuts. He was a top producer of peanuts in 1919. This 4-H club youth produced thirty-eight bushels of peanuts per acre and made sixty-five dollars on his prize-winning acre of peanuts.

Leila Mae Dukes, salad demonstration. Walton County, 1929.

university, but this weeklong event was designed just for boys. Extension faculty taught the boys new agricultural techniques and showed them pioneering research. When they went home, the boys would often apply what they learned and influenced how their family farms operated.

Meanwhile, at FAMU, the Negro Farm Boys' and Girls' State 4-H Club Short Course was first held in 1928. Eighty-two boys and girls were selected to participate in the very first short course. Unlike the other 4-H short courses at UF and FSCW, this one was coeducational, with

State Short Course for girls, 1925. Home demonstration in passé par touting, shower baths, and accessories.

First Boys' Short Course, 1916

Hillsborough County 4-H Club girls attend State 4-H Short Course at Florida A&M College, 1933.

boys and girls learning together. These short courses for boys and girls at UF, FSCW, and FAMU were the early forerunners of the event we know today as the Florida 4-H Congress.

The credit goes to the girls for starting the early forerunner of the State 4-H Council. The State Council of Home Demonstration work was the idea of Jocie Maddrey, a club girl from Alachua County. In 1919, when sixty-two

girls attended the State Short Course, they formed a state organization. Jocie was elected president, and Lois Hawkins of Quincy was elected secretary.

The Girls' State Council organization was formed before any of the county programs had a county council, but that soon changed. Only two years later, in 1921, Palm Beach County organized the first county council of home demonstration girls.

Among the boys, county and state councils emerged together. County councils for boys' club work were organized in Escambia, Hillsborough, Lake, Union, and Walton counties during the 1929–1930 club year. In 1930, a state council for boys was set up at the 1930 short course to promote club work throughout the Sunshine State. A state council for African-American girls was organized during the annual short course at FAMU in 1955.

Beginning in the late 1920s, Florida 4-H annually sent two boys and two girls to attend the National 4-H Club Camp, which was held on the mall in Washington, D.C. Tents were pitched near the Washington monument and 4-H members

National 4-H Club Camp, held in Washington, D.C., on the National Mall.

attended classes at the U.S. Department of Agriculture. Florida 4-H also sent a delegation annually to the National 4-H Club Congress, which was initially held in Chicago.

In 1927, twenty African-American 4-H members attended an interstate meeting of the Southern Negro Boys' and Girls' 4-H Camp at Tuskegee, Alabama. Three girls and three boys selected on the basis of outstanding records in project work and leadership attended the first Negro 4-H Camp at Baton Rouge, Louisiana, in 1948.

19

THE GREAT OUTDOORS
FLORIDA 4-H'S CAMPING PROGRAMS

Summer camp has been an important part of 4-H programs in Florida throughout its history. In 1919, boys from Clay County, led by Agent W. T. Nettles, enjoyed their first camping trip at Kingsley Lake. The next year, 4-H boys and girls from Polk County camped together at Wimauma, while Santa Rosa County boys and girls camped at Floridatown. The lack of equipment, poor locations for campgrounds, and fleas, redbugs, and mosquitoes caused Extension leaders to look for a better camping solution.

While traveling in northwest Florida with R. W. Blacklock, J. Lee Smith wrote that he "wished there was a place in west Florida with suitable accommodations [where] club boys and girls could be taken for a week's camping each summer. And, it would be desirable to have it located on the bay, preferably the National Forest, clear away from all active centers." R. W. Blacklock replied, "It has not been long since the supervisors of the Choctawhatchee National Forest told me that there was an ideal spot for such a camp at White Point on Choctawhatchee Bay and that they would be

State 4-H Club Boys' and Girls' Council, Gainesville. From left to right, first row: Jimmy Cummings, president (Palm Beach); James Lee, vice-president (Santa Rosa); and Morriam Simmons, vice-president (St. Johns). Second row: Lonnie T. Davis, sergeant-at-arms (Madison), and Tommy Lawrence, secretary (Volusia). Third row: Martha Mayfield, recording secretary (Volusia), and Betty Hanson, treasurer (Lake). Fourth row: Esther DeVore, historian (Marion); Sandra Dennison, corresponding secretary (Orange); and Albert Rice, Jr., reporter (Gilchrist). Fifth row: Arthur Cushman, chairman policy committee (Clay), and Charles Clark, executive committee (Jackson).

Flag-raising ceremony at Camp Timpoochee, August 1, 1935. It was an impressive part of the early morning program every day at camp.

Junior Citrus Institute at 4-H Camp McQuarrie, 1956. The fertilizer panel answers questions submitted by the audience. From left to right are Fred P. Lawrence; Dr. James Nesmith (Lakeland); Dr. H. J. Reitz and Dr. H. W. Ford (Citrus Station); Dr. Paul F. Smith, USDA (Orlando); and Dr. A. E. Wilson (Plymouth).

glad to have someone build a camp there." Soon after that conversation, 4-H Camp Timpoochee became a reality, opening in 1926 as the first permanent 4-H camp in Florida.

Many 4-H boys and girls donated a chicken each to be sold to support the building of 4-H Camp Timpoochee, and J. Lee Smith traveled to northwest Florida on a train, picking up donated chickens from 4-H members who met the train when it stopped, and then sold the chickens to support the camp's construction. More than $500, a sizable sum in the mid-1920s, was raised this way by 4-H boys and girls. Additional donors

were recruited by R. W. Blacklock, and fourteen cottages, a dining hall, and an auditorium were constructed.

For thousands of Florida youngsters, 4-H camps provided a place to make new friends, learn new skills, and have fun. Camp McQuarrie opened in the Ocala National Forest in 1924, 4-H Camp Cherry Lake opened in 1938, and 4-H Camp Cloverleaf opened in 1950.

Shown here are 4-H'ers at Camp Doe Lake after integration, 1972.

African-American 4-H members initially camped at the district level using tents. In 1948, 4-H Camp Doe Lake, the first permanent 4-H camp for African-American 4-H club members, opened in the Ocala National Forest. Located on a thirty-acre lake, the camp could accommodate 130 campers per week.

In the late 1960s, 4-H camping programs were integrated, and all of the camps were shared by 4-H members of all races. Eventually, camps McQuarrie and Doe Lake fell into disrepair, and the buildings were turned over to the National Forest Service.

For many 4-H members, their days at 4-H camp carry a special affection. In 2000, camps Cherry Lake and Cloverleaf were almost closed during a state budget crisis. The intervention of thousands of 4-H members and the Florida 4-H Foundation saved the facilities from closure, and they continue to modernize and improve their services. Camps Timpoochee, Cherry Lake, Cloverleaf, and Ocala remain summer havens for thousands of Florida youth.

Campers and staff at the first Seminole Indian 4-H Club Camp at Camp Cloverleaf. From left to right, seated: Eddie Shore, Harley Jumper, Jr., Jimmy Scott Osceola, Connie Johns, Nellie Smith, and Elise Tommie. Standing: Billy Cypress, Dan Bowers, Calvin Jumper, Fred Montsdeoca, Rudy Osceola, Mrs. Edith Boehmer, Raymond Cypress, Mitchell Cypress, Miss Lena Sturges, Polly Buck, Augustina Gopher, Jimmie Cummings, Elsie Johns, Willie Gopher, Jr., Dave Knight, J. D. Norton, Jr., Lawana Osceola, Rosie Billie, Hilton Cook, David Billie, David Jumper, Ben Floyd, Jesse Osceola, Fred Osceola, Jim Shore, and Richard Smith.

FACING TURBULENCE & CHANGE
THE 1960s

As the 1960s opened, it became increasingly difficult to run 4-H clubs through the schools. Woodrow W. Brown wrote in the 1963 Annual Report:

Overcrowded classrooms and the requirement for a high total number of minutes of academic instruction per day has caused our 4-H program to become a burden on the principals and teachers. There were just not enough minutes per day. This condition had become more apparent year after year. We were required to meet in basements, storerooms, and hallways. Meeting time was cut from one hour to forty-five minutes, then to thirty minutes. It was obvious, to maintain prestige and good name of 4-H, we must leave our school homes and establish ourselves within the community life in which the members lived.

Society was also changing and segregation was no longer permissible. The school-based 4-H clubs were abandoned in 1964, and were replaced with volunteer-led community or project clubs. This changed the role of the 4-H agent in Florida dramatically. It also empowered the 4-H club leader to take on a more active and engaged mentoring and teaching role with young people. The clubs would now meet in the local community and were led by volunteer 4-H club leaders.

It was a learning experience for everyone. The state 4-H staffs from the University of Florida and the Florida State College for Women were combined.

Some of the girls find out how to make storage boxes for doss and ends that litter the home in a household management course taught by Miss Catharine Knar, management specialist from the home demonstration department at FSU. From left to right are Margaret Shuler of Ocala. Miss Knarr, Gale Hergenroether of Orlando, and Elaine Reagan of Bradenton. June 14, 1961.

Home demonstration agents with clothing poster

Demonstration team at State Fair, 1962

Governor Faris Bryant receives a report on 4-H club work from 4-H members Jack Strickland and Janice Eubanks, 1960s. (FSU News Bureau photo by Ken Richards)

The merger melded 4-H programs serving boys and girls, African-Americans and Caucasians, into one state 4-H program. At the county level, separate programs for African-American, Native American, and Caucasian boys and girls were also merged.

It was a period of significant change for all Americans, with massive changes happening in politics, civil rights, and education. The state 4-H faculty devoted considerable effort in the late 1960s to dealing with the impacts of these changes and training county 4-H agents on volunteer management. Between 1964 and 1981, the number of 4-H volunteers grew to about 4,000 adults.

State 4-H events became fully co-educational in 1964, with the first 4-H club Congress held on the University of Florida campus. The short courses for boys and girls were discontinued. African-American youth attended the club Congress for the first time in 1966. Louise Brown remembered it as a pivotal moment for her husband Woodrow and said that the state staff wanted "those youngsters to feel the most welcomed."

The separate girls' and boys' State 4-H Councils were combined into one State 4-H Council with eight officers in 1964. Eddie Taylor of Clay County served as the first Florida 4-H Council president. The Florida 4-H Council met annually at the 4-H Congress until 1975, when additional changes were made. The Florida 4-H Council that year began meeting at the State Teen Leadership Forum in June. Later, this was changed to the third meeting of the State 4-H Executive Board.

In June 1963, thanks to planning by Woodrow Brown, Emily King, Joe Busby, and others, the Florida 4-H Foundation was founded. This direct support organization would play an important

Members of 4-H with Woodrow W. Brown at the 1971 Florida 4-H Congress.

role in recruiting and identifying private donors to support 4-H. Funds contributed through the foundation have helped 4-H members go to college, supported new public awareness efforts for 4-H, funded new 4-H programs, helped hundreds of 4-H'ers attend National 4-H Congress and National 4-H Conference, and recognized countless 4-H members for their outstanding achievements.

Following Mr. Brown's tenure as state 4-H leader, Dr. Jim Brasher led the 4-H program beginning in 1972. His job title was changed to assistant dean and department chair and he served as Extension's program leader for the statewide Florida 4-H Youth Development Program and as chair of an academic department within UF's Institute of Food and Agricultural Sciences. This position gave 4-H greater support within the Extension family of programs.

25

NEW PROGRAMS BEGIN
& 4-H FLOURISHES

During the 1970s, the Florida 4-H program flourished with the addition of many new programs that appealed to the interests of young people.

One of the most successful new programs was Florida 4-H Legislature, a mock youth Legislature conducted in Tallahassee in the State Capitol Building. The youth stayed in dormitories on the Florida State University campus and conducted a mock Legislature using the statehouse chambers, voting systems, and titles. Eventually, the program evolved to where youth could play out the roles of being a lobbyist for a particular cause, a legislator advocating for a bill, or a reporter in the press corps covering the event.

County and state faculty also began working again with public schools. They offered 4-H school enrichment programs that taught children public speaking, water conservation, food and nutrition, and much more. Greater focus was also placed on making the 4-H program accessible to all youth regardless of racial, economic, or rural/urban status. The 4-H Expanded Food and Nutrition Education Programs involved thousands of inner-city youth in 4-H programs, and also helped many low-income families improve their diets and exercise.

In 1981, Dr. Sue Fisher became the assistant dean and department chair for 4-H. The 4-H volunteer system grew to nearly 20,000 adult and teen leaders. Fundraising during the 1980s focused primarily on support for the development of the 4-H camps. In 1983, the Florida 4-H Foundation signed a lease with the U.S. Forest Service for 4-H Camp Ocala, located in the Ocala National Forest.

More than 1,500 youth and adults from across the state participated alongside faculty, donors, supporters, and County Extension agents in strategic planning in 1991–1992. The plan they developed served as a guide for programming and organizational development for 4-H. Based on recommendations in the plan and in response to budget constraints, considerable attention was given to updating the 4-H curriculum.

26

Judging, 1979–1980

Florida 4-H Legislature on the Capitol steps

View of the flagpole and lake at Camp Ocala

4-H FACES NEW CHALLENGES
AND RESPONDS

During the 1990s, downsizing at the University of Florida's Institute of Food and Agricultural Sciences impacted the 4-H Youth Development Program. The number of state-supported faculty at the state level were reduced. At the same time, the number of county 4-H agents increased due to financial support from county resources, so the 4-H programs were expanding rapidly.

On July 1, 1996, Florida 4-H experienced another major change when the Department of Family, Youth and Community Sciences was formed, merging the faculty within the Department of Home Economics with the faculty from the Department of 4-H and Other Youth Programs. The new department houses a multi-disciplinary faculty with assignments in areas of family and consumer sciences and youth and community development.

Florida State Fair Fashion Show, 2008. Best of Show winners, from left to right: Haley Gerig of Highlands County, Faith Mantia of St. Johns County, and Oksana Hammonds of Highlands County.

The state 4-H faculty focused their time and program leadership roles on liaisons with subject matter departments and specialists, while also developing a sizable committee structure to stay in touch with the county programs. Despite these challenges, 4-H continued to grow and served nearly a quarter of a million youth in Florida by 1997.

In January 1998, Damon Miller, Sr. assumed the role of assistant dean for 4-H programs at UF. In 2001, thousands of 4-H members participated in county "conversations" about the future of youth development in their communities. Through these

Youth and adults of 4-H work together to build youth-adult partnerships at the Learning and Leading Training, 2005.

interactive discussions around contemporary key issues facing young people, 4-H forged new ties with other youth-serving agencies and built consensus with community partners. Priorities identified at the county level were discussed and voted on at the State Conversation on Youth Development in January 2002, and carried forward to the National Conversation on Youth Development.

Promoting the University of Florida IFAS Extension 4-H Program in Tallahassee, Florida. From left to right are UF mascot "Al," Danielle Padgett, Bryan Russell, and UF mascot "Alberta."

Polk County 4-H Agent Nicole Walker teaches youth how to make a healthy snack. Florida State Fair, 2008.

Youth-adult partnership was an influence on State 4-H Council programming during this time period, with youth taking on a stronger leadership role. Staff and faculty served as mentors and advisors. In 1997, Florida 4-H and the Florida 4-H Foundation joined other state 4-H programs in supporting a national public service advertising campaign themed "Are You Into It?" that showed 4-H as a place to have fun, make friends, and volunteer to help others. The nationally placed radio, television, and print ads secured millions of dollars of donated advertising time in the Sunshine State, and the media focused new attention on 4-H service projects.

Volunteer screening and child protection practices were instituted, with special training and policy changes being introduced throughout the state. A statewide campaign to recruit more volunteers to the 4-H program was also launched in partnership with the Florida Department of Agriculture and Consumer Services.

In 2002, Dr. Marilyn Norman became the state 4-H leader, and she remains committed to 4-H's heritage as well as the future of the organization. In 2006, a special funding appropriation returned district 4-H agents to the state 4-H staff, and provides additional support to county 4-H programs.

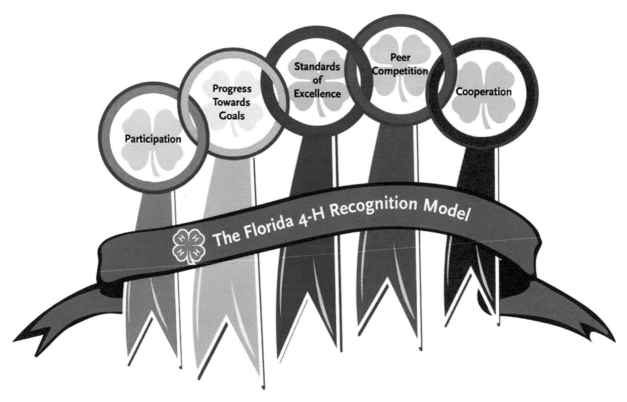

Florida 4-H Recognition Model

Governance of the Florida 4-H program is under the guidance of the 4-H Program Development Committee, which is made up of 4-H agents and state specialists working in partnership with Goal/Focus Teams. The Recognition for Excellence Program was completely revitalized. New partnerships formed with military installations and National Guard units across Florida have brought 4-H to more young people. Youth leadership training and healthy living initiatives have continued to expand 4-H's impact on young people today.

Since 1908, Florida 4-H has helped young people develop a love for lifelong learning, leadership skills, and self-confidence. What began as a program to teach new farming techniques became a community-based educational program that taught young people how to learn by doing and become engaged citizens. These 4-H programs have impacted the lives of countless Floridians for the better.

FLORIDA 4-H
CAMPING

4-H CAMP TIMPOOCHEE

Ready for a plunge in Choctowhatchee Bay. Camp Timpoochee, August 1935.

32

Established in 1926, Camp Timpoochee is Florida's oldest camping facility and one of the oldest residential camping facilities in the nation. Funding for the camp came partially in the form of materials donated by local businesses, partly from monetary donations from private citizens, and largely from the fundraising efforts of 4-H youth. In recognition of their efforts, 4-H'ers were asked to name the camp. Rusty Grundin, a Santa Rosa County 4-H'er, suggested the name of a chief from the Eulee tribe—a Native American tribe who befriended English settlers in Northwest Florida. The chief's name was Timpoochee Kinard.

Camp Timpoochee has undergone a number of renovations over the years. It wasn't until 1984 that major renewal efforts began, but this resulted in the construction of brand new cabins. Two years later, a pavilion was erected that overlooked the bay, and following the damage from Hurricane Opal, the beach was replenished and older buildings were given a "face lift."

Camp Timpoochee's unique location on the shores of the Choctawhatchee Bay made it the perfect location for marine science study. In 1998, a marine center was built that helps bring science to life for campers and adults. The living laboratory houses a number of 50- to 250-gallon aquariums where freshwater, bay, and gulf life can be seen up close and personal.

Campers at Camp Timpoochee discover the native wildlife.

4-H CAMP CHERRY LAKE

Camp Cherry Lake has the most unusual of beginnings. Cherry Lake was founded in 1937 by the Florida Rural Rehabilitation Corporation (FRRC).

During the Great Depression, President Roosevelt and Congress approved a plan that allowed for a joint federal-state relief effort to help get citizens back to work. The Federal Emergency Relief Administration (FERA) was established to oversee the State Emergency Relief Administration (SERA) that would be responsible for dividing up the federal monies appropriately. Part of Florida's plan to get its people back to work was to establish the FRRC. The FRRC bought the area now known as Cherry Lake, Florida, and subdivided it into forty- to sixty-acre plots of farmland. These plots were then mortgaged to local farmers. However, a section of the community on its lake was not mortgaged. This section, situated on the west side of Cherry Lake, became what campers, staff, and

Girls' 4-H craft class. Cherry Lake, July 23, 1948.

adults now consider home for five days and four nights every summer: 4-H Camp Cherry Lake.

Camp Cherry Lake was officially deeded to the 4-H clubs in Florida in 1967, and every summer since then, young boys and girls have looked forward to exploring and interacting with nature in a way that can only be done at camp.

33

Groundbreaking for a new adult cabin at Camp Cherry Lake. From left to right are: Diann Douglas, Dr. Larry Arrington, Dr. Marilyn Norman, Dr. John Woeste, and Shawn Baltzell.

4-H CAMP OCALA

A volunteer teaches the proper way to paddle at Camp Ocala.

34

Youth in 4-H learn teambuilding skills while at Camp Ocala.

Camp Ocala became one of Florida 4-H's residential camping facilities in 1983, when the University of Florida signed the lease with the National Forest Service. Once the lease was signed, programs began running immediately.

Camp Ocala is the largest of Florida's 4-H camps and provides camp-goers with the ability to "get away from it all." Its location in the heart of the Ocala National Forest allows campers to experience the true beauty of nature at its finest: untouched.

4-H CAMP CLOVERLEAF

The land that officially became 4-H Camp Cloverleaf was donated to the State of Florida in 1948. Construction didn't begin until a few years later, and camp was officially established in the year 1957.

Camp Cloverleaf sits on the banks of Lake Francis in Lake Placid, Florida. The first 4-H'ers ever to attend Camp Cloverleaf paid their way in eggs, chickens, corn, and many other agricultural products that were used during the week of camp.

Those who participated in the Camp Cloverleaf dedication get together around the base of the flagpole. From left to right are: Willard M. Fifield, provost for agriculture; Dr. J. Wayne Reitz, president, University of Florida; David Manley, Polk County; Don Deadwyler, Highlands County; Kay Christian, Broward County; Dr. Ralph L. Miller, chairman, State Board of Control; Hon. Doyle E. Carlton, Jr., state senator from Wauchula; Miss Phyllis Williamson, Sumter County; W. R. Hancock, Groveland, president, Florida Agricultural Council; L. S. McMullen, district agent and chairman of the finance committee; and Dr. Marshall O. Watkins, director, Florida Agricultural Extension Service. June 28, 1957.

A camp counselor teaches a camper how to shoot an arrow at Camp Cloverleaf.

4-H CAMP McQUARRIE
4-H CAMP DOE LAKE

36

Girls at 4-H Camp McQuarrie enjoy boat rides as well as swimming, June 25, 1940.

Little is known about the history of 4-H Camp McQuarrie and 4-H Camp Doe Lake. Camp McQuarrie was located in the Ocala National Forest and records indicate that the camp operated from 1939 to 1966. Camp Doe Lake, located in Marion County, Florida, was one of 4-H's residential camping facilities from 1949 to 1972. These camps served as training centers for new 4-H agents and provided accommodations to the African-American 4-H'ers who wanted a residential camping experience.

Members of 4-H ham it up for the camera at Camp Doe Lake.

These 4-H girls pledge allegiance as the flag is raised at Doe Lake, August 4, 1949.

FLORIDA 4-H

COUNTY HISTORIES

ALACHUA COUNTY
BY: RONDA BANNER

The Alachua County 4-H Program has played an important role in the history of 4-H in Florida. Alachua, Marion, and Bradford counties were the first three programs started in 1909. Started as "corn clubs," they were the precursor to the 4-H clubs that we know and love today.

Alachua County also played an important role in the foundation of the State 4-H Council. It was the idea of a former Alachua County Girls' Club president, Jocie Maddrey, in 1919. She presented the idea and was elected as the first State Girls' Club Council president. The girls' and boys' club State Councils merged in later years to form what is now known as the State 4-H Council.

The first 4-H agent in Alachua County was J. J. Vernon, who was also the dean of the College of Agriculture at the University of Florida.

Major programs in the early years of the program included agriculture and home economics. Today, programs still follow the traditional history, with the additions of popular projects like horse, livestock, and gardening. A strong emphasis on citizenship and leadership has come to the forefront in recent years as well. School enrichment clubs are also popular, with subject matter ranging from gardening to embryology.

The longest-running club in Alachua County is Alachua Rope and Halter. It was founded in 1982 by the families of Bob and Pam Sands and John and Pat Sands. It is still in existence today and still has a strong emphasis on agriculture and livestock.

Many winning horse teams have come out of Alachua County, including the 1981 team consisting of Hillary Mullins, Mary Hill, Ed Johnson from the state office, Susan Sumner, and Greg Ott.

39

Enrollment numbers have fluctuated over the years, but currently, the county boasts over 400 traditional 4-H members, with another 1,500 members in school enrichment programs. The county averages 2,500 to 3,000 kids in all phases of the program.

There have been many accomplishments on the part of Alachua County 4-H'ers over the years, including state honors in the areas of horse judging, meat judging, poultry judging, land judging, and livestock judging.

The first organized 4-H horse show was organized by All Breeds 4-H Club back in the 1960s. In 1972, the Alachua County 4-H Horse Council was formed and still organizes and coordinates county horse shows and county horse-related events today. Alachua County 4-H'ers are well represented in all aspects of the horse project and consistently have members showing at the State 4-H Show and participating on horse teams.

Citizenship has played an important role in Alachua County 4-H as well. In 1978, the Micanopy 4-Hoofs 4-H Club received top honors in the state for their Community Pride Project for landscaping the Micanopy Town Hall. In following years, they were also honored for building a community park, landscaping the Micanopy Fire Station, building community bulletin boards and picnic tables, as well as providing window screens for the Town Hall.

Ronda Ott, State 4-H Council president (1983–1984), accepts a National Conference trip from Dr. Woeste.

The Micanopy Friendship 4-H Club continues the legacy started many years ago, and is now helping to renovate the community park that was originally built by Micanopy 4-Hoofs with an interactive Butterfly Garden.

Alachua County has had a legacy of leadership over the last century. In 1981, Alachua County 4-H member and State Council President Greg Ott was recognized on the national level as one of six 4-H'ers nationwide to receive the Presidential Tray Award for his leadership and citizenship skills in his community and 4-H projects. His sister, Ronda Ott, served as State Council secretary in 1981–1982 and State Council president in 1983–1984

with fellow Alachua County 4-H'er Jan Richardson as State Council reporter. Jan also served as State Council vice president in 1984–1985.

Several Alachua County 4-H'ers have had the honor of participating in National 4-H Conference, including Greg Ott in 1981, Ronda Ott in 1983, and Elizabeth Eccleston in 2003. Many Alachua County 4-H'ers have also been chosen to participate in National 4-H Congress and received 4-H scholarships towards their college education.

Alachua County 4-H'ers have promoted the program in their community by participating in the University of Florida Homecoming Parade for the last twenty-five years. Each year, the float and

Then and Now—Alachua County 4-H'ers have participated in the University of Florida homecoming parade for the last twenty-five years. The county float started out on a small county flatbed, and is now built on a huge IFAS semi-trailer flatbed.

interest in it gets bigger and better. What started out as a small flatbed trailer has grown into a huge float built on an IFAS semi-trailer.

Alachua County continues to serve an important role in the formation of Florida 4-H history. With its close proximity to the University of Florida, it has had the honor of starting pilot programs, including Operation Military Kids, and looks forward to making history for the 4-H program for the next one hundred years.

41

BAKER COUNTY

Baker County 4-H is a rural program. In 2007, 121 youth members were enrolled in 147 4-H projects. There were eight 4-H clubs in Baker County and twenty-two adult volunteers. Major projects in 2007 were swine, horse, and beef projects.

Boy showing his hog project.
Baker County Fair, 2007.

Livestock Judging Team. Florida State Fair, 2008.

Horse Judging Team. South Florida Fair, 2008.

Baker County 4-H Horse Show, 2008.

42

BAY COUNTY
BY: PAULA DAVIS

In Bay County, 4-H began in 1954. The first agents were Horrace Carr and Emma Benton. The major programs at that time were school enrichment programs covering seasonal topics, home health, forestry, and livestock. Today, we have military programs, school enrichment, and community clubs with focuses on horses, gardening, marine science, photography, healthy lifestyles, public speaking, camping, and Operation Military Kids. Our longest-running club is the Riding Rebels, which began in the early 1960s and is still continuing as one of two horse clubs in the county. They have gone from having horses stabled at

the county fairgrounds to having horses at their own homes.

There are several distinguished 4-H alumni from Bay County: Dr. Reid Baughman of Baughman Chiropractic; Ellen Bylsma; Amy Bynum; John Bynam; Michelle Bryant, a traveling nurse; Casey Caldwell; Bill Carr; Carolyn Carr; Carol Collins, a pharmacist; Gail Kelley Cooper; Tara Fox, the 2003 National Barrel Horse Association Team 3D Champion Teen and a pharmacist; Doreen Geldert of the city of Panama City; Bobby Harding, Panama City Beach police chief; Ann Harrison; Helen

Five Florida 4-H club boys, who in May 1954 leased an acre of water to begin the first 4-H oyster project in the nation, are shown inspecting their "farming" site from the deck of a shrimp trawler. From left to right are: Donnie Wildman, Albert Hogan, Marshall Gore, Fred Waters, Bobby Seaborn, Bay County Agent J. A. Sorenson, and George H. Toepfer, Florida conservation agent, Salt Water Division.

Bay County Horse Show, 1982.

Harrison; Kim Pettis Martin; Debbie Mastro, a teacher; Cindy Morris; Anna Prevost, the principal of New Horizons Learning Center; Deanna Lepore; Beth Renfroe, a paraprofessional; Kathy Kaeding Rigdon; Ginger Spivey, a middle school teacher and show judge; Carol Roberts Waldo, from the Chamber of Commerce; and Barbara Utter, a teacher.

43

BRADFORD COUNTY

The rural Bradford County was one of the first counties to participate in the corn clubs and tomato clubs. Major programs in Bradford County are arts and crafts, swine, and outdoor education and recreation. In 2007, there were 202 members enrolled in 272 projects and forty-eight adult volunteers.

Corn club boy. Bradford County, July 11, 1913.

BREVARD COUNTY
BY: CYNTHIA MINOT

The earliest documentation of Brevard County 4-H dates back to 1916, when Mrs. Walter W. Gay worked as a home demonstration agent, teaching canning. There is a record of 4-H members, "tomato girls," growing and canning tomatoes in both Cocoa and Micco.

Citrus and cattle were the dominant industries in 1935 when Thomas Cain, Jr. and Eunice Gay were the agricultural and home demonstration agents. Monthly 4-H programs were conducted in all

Angela Barrelle's smile reflects the pride and tradition of the 4-H Beef Club, Brevard's longest continuously organized 4-H group, formed in 1972 by County Extension Director and Agriculture Agent Lowell Loadholtz. (Brevard 4-H photograph collection, circa 1984)

three of the county's high schools by the agents. Records from 1939 show 250 4-H girls, twelve 4-H clubs, three home demonstration women acting as 4-H leaders, and eight homes opened for 4-H meetings.

James Oxford (employed 1945–1971) and Sue Young (employed 1952–1975) became the next

Extension agents during an era that included the beginning of the space industry in Brevard.

Teenager Lynnie Finney's participation in Titusville High School's 4-H club in 1934 ultimately blossomed into her outstanding service as an adult 4-H volunteer leader. When Sue Young shared a pet dream of augmenting school 4-H clubs through small neighborhood youth groups, Lynnie formed the Banana River Girls 4-H Club

Sharon Jones demonstrates to a group of fascinated 4-H'ers the anatomy of the equine skeletal structure with her teaching aide, "Bones." The skeleton, assembled by Sharon, continues to be an instructional tool today. (Bette Jones photograph, 1974)

in 1953, which operated for at least seven years. This active club was featured in the *Progressive Farmer's Magazine*.

In 1967, there were seventy 4-H groups in the county. This is an outstanding number, especially

As rockets stand sentinel in Kennedy Space Center's "Rocket Garden," Extension 4-H Agent Gus Koerner prepares attentive Brevard 4-H members for a scavenger hunt assisted by GPS. (Cynthia Minot photograph, 2007)

Fifteen-year-old Melbourne teenager Bill Nelson, shown with mother Nannie Merle Nelson, poses with his prize, a Santa Gertrudis 4-H heifer named "Gussy." Nelson, an outstanding county, state, and national 4-H'er, achieved further success as a U.S. senator and NASA astronaut. As a teen, he was elected as the State 4-H Council treasurer and vice-president for boys. (Bill Nelson photograph collection, 1957)

at a time when 4-H enrollment across Florida had plummeted by 70 percent just three years earlier. The decline was the consequence of a 1965 state Extension mandate barring school 4-H clubs. This resulted in a switch to the community-based club system, primarily lead by volunteers. Brevard was a leader in the utilization of volunteer leaders.

In the mid-1970s, Joy Satcher (employed 1966–1993) was appointed as the county's very first 4-H agent. She served in this position until 1981. All of these early agents served for many years and were icons in the community due to the expansive reach and success of their programs.

The county 4-H Horse Program began under the instruction of Mrs. "Smitty" Hooper, in the late 1960s. The program, based at Moody's Ranch in Cocoa, allowed youth to pay for lessons and then ride in horse shows using the ranch's horses. The competitive Horse Program for youth who owned a horse began in 1970 or '71, when arrangements were made for 4-H points to be awarded through a show held at Hunt Acres in Cocoa. Three girls competed and were entitled to advance to state. In 1975, Brevard members captured the Horseman of the Year and second runner-up awards. A significant milestone occurred in the mid-1980s, when the program obtained property on north Merritt Island for a 4-H Equestrian Center. Volunteers cleared the property, built the arenas and buildings, and continue to maintain the facility today. Among the highlights of the program are nineteen years of horse judging teams coached by Barbara Nagle, which includes fourteen wins at the state competition and numerous top-five placings at the regional and national competitions.

Financial support garnered by the Brevard County 4-H Foundation has provided hundreds of youth and volunteers the opportunity to participate in camps, contests, and educational events. The Foundation began in the mid-1970s, was incorporated in 1999, and surpassed $100,000 in investments in 2007, the same year it introduced a $4,000 college scholarship.

Numerous grants have provided funding through the years. Grants enabled the creation of the Summer Education Program (SEP) for three years (1974–1976), where paid interns conducted a multitude of youth programs throughout the county. The success of the SEP convinced the county commission to fund three year-round 4-H program assistants. This staff expansion had an immense

Senator Bill Nelson

impact on the program's outreach and growth. Patricia Trautman (employed 1977–present), the current 4-H program assistant in Titusville, is the longest-serving Brevard Extension Service employee.

Grants have also allowed for the purchase of equipment such as canoes, shooting sports equipment, incubators, laptop computers, and G.P.S. receivers. Chevron's Community Pride Grants have allowed clubs to conduct dozens of service projects in the past three decades.

47

Today's program provides a blend of traditional and contemporary topics. Youth are still excited to be involved in plant and animal sciences, cooking, and sewing. Urban youth had the chance to raise livestock by using pens on-site at the Brevard County Sheriff's farm since the mid-'80s. More recently developed programs include geospatial, marine science, and rocketry. With so many topic choices, our specialty continues to be developing life skills, leadership, and citizenship.

BROWARD COUNTY
BY: JOE METELLUS

Broward County's 4-H Program began in 1939. Enrollment has changed over the years to include more inner-city youth and other members who may not have access to the traditional 4-H program that focuses primarily on agriculture. Major programs in Broward County include public speaking, leadership, financial literacy, environmental education, horticulture, companion animals, and horse projects.

The longest-running club is Project Stable 4-H Club. This club was started by Sandy and Shel McCartney in 1980. The club has changed names a couple of times, but continues to focus on horse projects. Two club alumni went on to become veterinarians. The Project Stable 4-H Club also is part of the Equestrian and Farm Program that works with special needs children and provides agricultural education to the general public.

The 4-H club. Daytona Beach, Florida, June 23, 1959.

Broward County would like to recognize two distinguished alumni, S. Kimara March, M.D. and Hunter Williams. S. Kimara March, M.D. is a senior medicine resident at the Mayo Clinic in Rochester, Minnesota. Dr. March has held numerous leadership positions in the past, including a state 4-H officer position in Florida, and has been recognized as a 4-H Alumni of the Year as well. Hunter Williams started his college education early by completing twelve college-level classes between fifth and ninth grade and taking thirteen advanced placement courses in high school. Williams was involved with many things, including 4-H, where he served as speaker of the house at Florida 4-H Legislature. He also drafted a bill that is currently in the Florida Legislature. He has earned many academic honors. Williams plans to major in international economics and East Asian language and literature.

49

CALHOUN COUNTY
BY: JUDY LUDLOW

The University of Florida Cooperative Extension Service has been an important part of the lives of many Calhoun County residents since the late 1920s. Calhoun County is a rural county in Florida's panhandle with a population of approximately 13,000. The 4-H programs that have existed over the years have encouraged youth to be all they can be. The goal of the 4-H program is to provide opportunities for youth to learn new skills that foster leadership, citizenship, personal achievement, and healthy growth in a fun, energized environment. Adult volunteers are crucial to the success of any 4-H program. Without adult volunteers, there would be no clubs or activities. In Calhoun County, there have been countless volunteer hours devoted to youth development since the program's inception. Reciprocally, the 4-H program provides adult volunteers from the community a place to share their time, skills, life experiences, and guidance with the youth of Calhoun County.

A Calhoun County 4-H'er is shown with her prize-winning beef project.

Proud winners of the August 1995 Calhoun County Junior Fashion Show

Of course, the Cooperative Extension Service 4-H agents are the program catalysts. The Calhoun County 4-H experience would not exist without their dedication, skill, and oversight. There are, unfortunately, no records of who the very first Calhoun County 4-H agent was. Mr. Harvey T. Paulk, Calhoun County Extension director from 1962 to 1972, provided a list of at least thirteen county agents that he was aware of, and in 1975, three program assistants were hired to provide home economics educational activities in Calhoun County.

Early in its history, the major 4-H activities in Calhoun County focused on homemaker clubs and activities in the schools. In 1975, the Calhoun County commissioners passed a resolution proclaiming October 5 through 11, 1975, as 4-H Week in Calhoun County. In that school year, there were 438 4-H members in thirteen different clubs. "Members participated in 29 individual project areas, including cooking, sewing, rabbits, public speaking, forestry, child development, small engines, veterinary science, dog care and training, and many other areas."

Recent clubs and activities have revolved around healthy eating and cooking, outdoor adventures, livestock, personal safety, the environment, and science. Enrollment numbers have fluctuated and are now far less than the 438 noted in 1975. There has been significant turnover of Calhoun County 4-H agents in the last five years. The future is encouraging, however, in that many adults who participated in 4-H in their youth are willing to volunteer for today's youth.

Florida's 4-H program has no doubt produced many successful alumni, and Calhoun County is no exception. It is difficult to track the lives of the many successful 4-H children of Calhoun County, but one, however, was recently honored with statewide recognition, and a second is a retired army colonel currently serving in Iraq. Mrs. Patty Melvin was raised in Blountstown and was a Calhoun County 4-H Club member in the fourth through sixth grades. She has volunteered with the Jackson County 4-H Program for more than ten years, dedicating her time as a club leader and positively influencing the lives of hundreds of youth. Because of her contributions, Mrs. Melvin was honored with the Florida 4-H Volunteer of the Year Award. Mr. Logan Barbee was also raised in Blountstown and was a Calhoun County 4-H member in the 1960s. He was the Calhoun County

Extension director from 1981 to 2006. Logan retired from the army with the rank of colonel special operations, and is currently serving in Iraq as senior executive advisor to the U.S. State Department.

Calhoun County 4-H also has an interesting connection with 4-H Camp Timpoochee's history. The camp, located on the Choctawhatchee Bay in the panhandle, was established as the first residential 4-H camping facility in Florida in 1926. Additionally, it was one of the first 4-H residential

Girls from 4-H teach about nutrition and careers.

camps in the nation. New cabins were built in 1984 with financial assistance from the Florida 4-H Foundation to replace the old rustic wood cabins. Logan Barbee was instrumental in securing and relocating those rustic Timpoochee cabins to the Calhoun County 4-H Youth Camp. These cabins are still in use, and in addition to camping, the Youth Camp provides numerous opportunities for activities for residents of Calhoun and its surrounding counties.

CHARLOTTE COUNTY
BY: JOAN KEENEY

Thirty-four years ago, in a small town on the west coast of Florida, something wonderful happened: 4-H came to Charlotte County. Little did anyone know at that time what an impact 4-H would have on so many families in the years to come.

The first 4-H organizational meetings were held in September 1974. Mrs. Pat Smith, Extension Home Economics Program leader, was in charge of the 4-H program. Some of the early clubs covered the following project areas: sewing, horse, clothing, dairy and beef cattle, child development, rabbits, swimming, woodworking, drama, cake decorating, dog and cat club, teen leadership, sailing, horticulture, and bicycle. With names like Charlotte Sherbets, Saddle Stradlers, Oreos, Trail Blazers, Skin Diving, Bugaroos, Easy Riders, Rabbit Raisers, Rowdy Rowdy Pipers, Silly Stitchers, and Kaleidoscope Teen Club, who wouldn't want to be in 4-H?

The 4-H program has come a long way since the '70s, but some things have stayed the same. There is still a beef club, a dairy club, a dog club, a horse club, a teen club, and a rabbit club, but there are also new clubs: scrap-booking, goats, livestock judging, theater arts, gardening, and pocket pets.

The longest-running club is the Cows 'n Plows 4-H Club. This club was formed in 1990 and remains strong. The purpose of this club is to teach youth about beef cattle, swine, and lambs. Margie Lewis and Ted Lynn led this club the first year, followed by Renee Toussaint. Miss Toussaint was the leader

52

Punta Gorda Club members, 1919

until 1993, when Becky Jones and Nancy Lee took over as leaders. Over the past fifteen years, these two dedicated ladies have helped, educated, and watched as young 4-H'ers turned into mature, upstanding citizens of the community.

Other 4-H clubs are: Fur 'n Feathers, Creative Croppers, Dairy Club, Eco Club, Everything Home Grown, Four Paws and a Tail, Just Kidding Goat Club, Manes 'n Reins, Mission Possible Teen Club, Lucky Charms, Pocket Pals, and Top Choice Livestock Judging.

In the thirty-four years that 4-H has been in Charlotte County, the most significant event took place in 2004. On August 13, 2004, Hurricane Charlie made a direct hit in Charlotte County. Buildings were destroyed, homes were ripped apart, and families were uprooted. For days, there was no way to contact anyone. There was no power, food, or water, but there was compassion for your neighbor. The community pulled together and made it through this event. The 4-H program was greatly affected by the hurricane because 4-H's main meeting building was now a pile of twisted metal and glass. Some families had to move because their homes were no longer livable. However, by November 2004, the 4-H program was back up and running thanks to the community and the dedicated volunteers of 4-H.

CITRUS COUNTY
BY: PATRICIA AND NIKKI UZAR

The first Citrus County "farm demonstrator," Walter E. Allen, received his first paycheck on April 5, 1915, for the amount of twenty-five dollars (BOCC minutes). That year, the first Citrus County Fair was held. It originated through the efforts of John E. King and Walter Allen. The fair was an open-air exhibit held in Lecanto (Hampton Dunn, *Back Home*). Other county fairs were held throughout the 1920s and '30s. These were primarily 4-H exhibits organized by the county and home demonstration agent.

From 1920 through the Depression era, Elizabeth W. Moore was the home demonstration agent. She arrived with her four-year-old son at the old hotel in Inverness. She placed her baggage on the floor and her .45-caliber pistol on the counter. No one questioned the single woman with her "hardware" (Dunn).

Mary (Landrum) Harrison remembers Elizabeth Moore coming to lead 4-H at the Pleasant Grove School once a month. Mrs. Harrison remembers making a 4-H quilt and going to Camp McQuarrie. "We rode all day to get there. It felt like we were going to New York City it was so far away." Mrs. Harrison also recalls, "One time the 'original Charlie Dean' allowed Ms. Moore to take us, by boat, to camp at his island on the Chassawitksa River."

Alma "Shortie" Bedford started the Floral City 4-H Club in 1958. She says, "I remember we first met at the Methodist Church across from the [Old Floral City] school, and then moved to the fire department. Them were the good ole days." Shortie's son, Gene, remembers that Quentin Medlin "taught them how to do surgery on the chickens, so they would grow bigger."

Mrs. Frances Rooks is part of several generations of 4-H involvement. Frances's mother, Annie VanNess Croft, was a leader of a "Tomato Club" in 1932. Annie taught the girls cooking and canning.

53

Citrus County 4-H girls at Camp McQuarrie, 1936, under the leadership of Mrs. Elizabeth W. Moore, county home demonstration agent (back row, far left).

Also, Frances relates a story of a friend's mother, Eloise Lewis, who traveled in 1915 from Floral City by train to Inverness to meet the Extension agent, Walter E. Allen. Then they traveled together to the Lecanto "livestock building, [where the fair was held] to do a 4-H speech contest." Mrs. Moore taught Frances Rooks to make ginger snap cookies as a 4-H'er herself at Hernando School.

Mrs. Rooks began the 4-H Inverness Club that met during class at the Inverness grammar school. Later, the club moved to the "lounge room" of the Florida Power Building. Frances was an assistant leader in 1970 to Mr. Fisher, who led, with eight members, Circle C Bar-I. Following this, Frances led the club until 1978, when Mrs. Cybil Barco took over until 1981.

Mrs. Rooks's children, Ella and Larry, joined 4-H. Larry Rooks was involved in Mr. Quentin Medlin's— the agricultural agent from 1947 through 1974— Gardening Club and later in Ease's Rough Riders (ERR). Ella Rooks Thomas was involved in the grammar school 4-H group. Ella's children Martha Thomas and Sarah Hensley were members of ERR as youths. Both girls have careers as agents; Martha as livestock in Lake, and Sarah as 4-H in Sumter County.

Any history of Citrus 4-H must feature Mrs. Eloise VanNess, with seventy-two years of 4-H involvement to date. Mrs. Eloise camped in 1937 and attended the 4-H girls' "short course around 1940 in Tallahassee." Later, Mrs. Eloise started as a 4-H volunteer in 1958 and began the Citrus County 4-H Horse Club.

Mr. Hal Porter joined Mrs. Eloise's 4-H club at nine years old. In 1965, the club's name was changed when "Mr. VanNess called his wife Ease, short for Eloise." The club then became Ease's Rough Riders. After graduation, Hal worked for the state 4-H office for Dr. James Brasher. Hal says, "My dearest friendships [through 4-H], which I treasured, are Dr. Hal Phillips from Williston and Brian Putnal, Mayo." Hal continues to serve 4-H as

the Citrus County 4-H Foundation president and as the fair manager "to pay back for what I benefited in the 4-H program."

There are seventeen 4-H clubs that range from fifty-year longevity to just recently formed. Our longest-running club is Ease's Rough Riders 4-H Club, with Eloise VanNess as club founder and a leader since 1958. The club began as a horse club going on trail rides on the Flying Eagle Ranch and hosting benefit county horse shows. Around the late 1970s, when Ginger Whitton, one of Mrs. Eloise's daughters, was leader, the club diversified by adding other livestock projects for the county fair. Another relative, Christine VanNess Waller, is currently a leader with Kara and Michael Coover, Ella Thomas, and Marlena Welch.

National 4-H Week, 2007, was celebrated in Citrus County by a Board of County Commissioners Proclamation on October 9, 2007. Those present at the meeting that day, from left to right, were: Amy Duncan, Daniel Gandee, Josh Dovi, David Dovi, and Jonathan Dovi of American Eagles 4-H Club; Jenny Frank, Monica Frank, Peter Uzar, Chrissy Uzar, and Nikki Uzar of Floral City Team Green; and Citrus County BOCC Chairman Dennis Damato. Amy Duncan has been the 4-H agent since August of 2001. She strives to keep 4-H a "top-notch youth development organization" through public recognition such as this Proclamation, continued support of traditional 4-H club projects, and new special interest programs like 4-H Culinary Camp. (Photographer Jessica Lambert)

CLAY COUNTY
BY: LISA ROWAND

The earliest 4-H reference in Clay County was in 1935, mainly regarding home demonstration Extension agents. Beulah Phelps was a home demonstration agent from 1935 to 1942. Elizabeth Starbird was a home demonstration agent from 1942 to 1946, when the program was discontinued. The program was reinstated in 1950.

Jesse Godbold was the Extension director from 1971 to 1996. He came to Clay from Liberty County in 1971, and was known as "the man who could really get things done."

Muriel Turner took over as Extension director after Godbold retired in 1996. Turner was hired as a home economics agent in 1991. She served as interim agriculture agent when Godbold retired.

The first Clay County Fair was held in 1987. Mr. Claude Kelly is known as the "Father of the Clay County Fair," and is also the founding father of the Clay County 4-H Foundation. He established the Foundation in 1980 with the main function of soliciting donations from corporations or individuals to provide scholarships for Clay County youth to attend district, regional, state, and national events. The Clay County 4-H Foundation is still provides scholarships today for county youth.

Two publications exist in Clay County: the 4-H newsletter called the *Clover Connection* and the *Clay County Contact*. The *Clover Connection* was formerly known as the *Green Sheet* and was changed in approximately 1998. It is published by the Extension Office. The *Clay County Contact* is also published by the Extension Office and includes articles about 4-H, lawns and shrubs, vegetables and plants, family and consumer sciences, and agricultural

The Achiever's 4-H Club works the 4-H booth for County Council.

Clay County Legislature Trip. Tallahassee, Florida, 1999.

Dylan Johnson and Tristan Rowand. Clay County Fair, April 14, 2007.

management in each issue. The *Contact* celebrated its tenth anniversary in 2008.

The longest-running clubs in Clay are The Achievers, Clay Hunters, the Marine Club, and Prime Cuts. Roger Farrell has been involved with the Marine Club for almost twenty years. Prior to that, he was involved with the shooting sports club. Liz Burris took over The Achievers from Diane James in 1990 and then turned the club over to Lisa Rowand in 2004. Burris has been the leader of The Legislature Program for many years. Diane and Glenn Lassiter are still active in leading Prime Cuts 4-H Club after nearly twenty years.

Over the last ten to twelve years, the overall number of youth enrolled in Clay County 4-H has dropped. Current members are enrolled in a wide variety of projects from poultry to rocketry.

Even with a numbers drop, the Clay County 4-H Program is still going strong. The towns included in Clay County are Keystone Heights, Middleburg, Orange Park, Grandin, and Green Cove Springs. The county has a population of roughly 178,000 and about 240 youth are enrolled in 4-H in fifteen different clubs. The Achievers is a general interest club led by Lisa Rowand of Keystone Heights.

Kick 'n' UP Heels Club is led by Donna Diehl of Middleburg, and is also a general interest club. The Marine Club is led by Liz Stone and Roger Farrell of Green Cove Springs. The livestock interest clubs are Clay High Farm Team led by Carole Woods of Green Cove Springs, Prime Cuts led by Diane and Glenn Lassiter of Middleburg, and the Ham Jammers led by Becky Smith of Green Cove Springs. The majority of the clubs in Clay are horse clubs. They are Clay Hunters led by Cindy Hicks of Grandin, Pony Express led by Rose Leverette of Middleburg, and Steaming Saddles led by Colleen Potter of Middleburg. The Legislature Program is led by Liz Burris of Keystone Heights. And last but not least, there are a few clubs that are primarily made up of homeschoolers. They are Creative Clover led by Stacia Harper of Green Cove Springs, Treasure Seekers led by Patti Crawford of Keystone Heights, and the Wranglers led by Sue Anne Rubright of Orange Park, Florida.

Current events include a carnival at the Northeast Florida Jumping for 4-H event sponsored by the North Florida Hunter Jumper Association in January. Most of the clubs participate in the St. Johns River Cleanup in March. County events also held in March include demonstrated or illustrated talks, public speaking, Fashion Revue, and Share-the-Fun. During April, the fair comes to town and all of the clubs participate. The Legislature Program members attend Legislature in Tallahassee in late June to see how bills are passed into laws. Several clubs also send members to County Camp at 4-H Camp Ocala in late June or early July. Leaders attend training sessions at Rock Eagle 4-H Center in October. In December, youth from several clubs compete in a Holiday Bake-off.

COLLIER COUNTY
BY: DANEILLE STEWART AND LINDA DENNING

The Collier County 4-H Program began in the 1950s and is known for its long-standing, over-achieving, totally committed Extension agents. Over the last fifty years, there have only been three agents, Donald W. Lander, Dallas Townsend, and Linda Denning. Currently at the helm is a very young and energetic Anna Galdames, who said, "If I follow in their footsteps I should retire before age 60!"

Don Lander was the first 4-H agent and then Extension director, spanning thirty years. The Extension Office was in Everglades City until Hurricane Donna hit, when they were moved to East Naples. Mr. Lander was a driving force in building Camp Cloverleaf. He organized boys and took them on Collier County's first camping trip. Lander convinced county commissioners to finance a new cabin at Cloverleaf, and he also got C. J. Jones Lumber Company to donate the lumber for the other buildings. As CED, he was

actively involved in camp. When he retired, 4-H leaders gave him a lifetime pass to 4-H camp!

Dallas Townsend became the 4-H agent/livestock agent when Mr. Lander became Extension director. He started community 4-H clubs, emphasizing leadership and public speaking. His 4-H members became adept at demonstrations and speaking skills. He trained many winning judging teams that competed at state and national events. He later became the Extension director in Hendry County.

Meats Judging Team, first place, July 31, 1978. From left to right are Roger Watson, Bart Townsend, Jimmy Crew, and Richard Lockerby.

Camp Cloverleaf, July 1981

Several livestock agents served after him, most notably Kevin Hill, who served for fifteen years supporting livestock and horse programs.

In 1976, Linda Denning started her thirty-year career with Collier County 4-H as a paraprofessional, charged with expanding 4-H audiences according to affirmative action guidelines. Soon, she had all third-graders completing the 4-H Seed Project. In 1977, she became the 4-H agent. Denning established Collier County's 4-H Club Foundation in 1978, with leadership and donations from civic clubs, businesses, and individuals, and later the Collier County United Way, which now funds outreach programs. Carl Fruectemeyer of Marco Island was the first president. Grants funded environmental projects including Earth Connections, Eyes on the Environment Program, and Family Marine Nights. The 4-H club partnered with the YMCA, Boys' and Girls' Clubs, Rookery Bay, NAACP, libraries, parks, and schools. An anonymous donation funded the 4-H Children's Garden at the Horticultural Learning Center. The Farm City BBQ began in the 1960s and has become a major fundraising event.

The Extension Office was in the Collier County Courthouse, and teens visiting the county offices knew little about local government. Mrs. Denning started The Know Your County Government

Program in 1979, partnering with the Collier County League of Women Voters and the Collier County Public Schools social studies department. This became a feeder program with additional intensive training and scholarships for 4-H Legislature, where Collier youth excelled, winning many Chris Allen awards and serving on and chairing the State 4-H Legislature Committee. Annual club officer training was taught by teen county council members, many of whom became state officers. Scholarships were also provided for Citizenship Washington Focus.

The longest-running club is Immokalee Livestock, organized under the direction of Dallas Townsend in 1968 by Audrey Johnson. As a 4-H leader, a founding Collier County 4-H Foundation board

Immokalee 4-H leaders with Livestock Agent Kevin Hill and 4-H Coordinator Linda Denning (far right), at the satellite Extension Office in Immokalee. Leaders are: (back row) Maria Lucera, Claudette Gillings, Audrey Johnson, (front row) Brenda Houser, Jean Smith, Mrs. Garrett, and April Garrett.

member, and Collier County Fair manager in the 1980s and 1990s, Mrs. Johnson always put children's needs first. Thanks to her, an entire generation benefited from 4-H club participation, and many serve as active leaders and parents today. The club's primary focus is livestock with an emphasis on community service.

Denise Coleman (later Blanton) was the first home economics agent, joined by Jan Bennett in 1977 and Bonnie Fauls in 1978. All contributed to 4-H Family and Consumer Sciences programs, including consumer judging, sewing workshops, Fashion Revue, and coordinating the family and community educators (formerly Extension homemakers). The homemakers greatly supported 4-H county and district events, the fair, the Farm City BBQ, sewing workshops, school programs, YMCA programs, etc., and provided camp scholarships. Key homemakers were Jo Selvia, Wynn Somers, and Ann Hoskins.

Alumni of 4-H from around the nation moved to Collier County and contributed to 4-H in important ways. Judy Keller of Ohio served as Foundation president and Nancy Alward Roberts of New Hampshire has been a consistent donor since 1981. Warren Schmidt, retired senior officer (Youth Programs) of the Food and Agricultural Organization of the United Nations, assisted with volunteer training and teen recreational leadership training, chaired the 4-H county coordinating committee, and served on the 4-H Foundation board. He presented his slides of "4-H Around the World." Locally, Mary Leon was a 4-H member in Marion County and volunteered in Collier County. She organized The Parker Perry Patches, Leon's Leaders, and Shadowlawn Seahawks 4-H clubs, reaching hundreds of children in racially mixed neighborhoods by recruiting an integrated group of adult leaders. A dedicated woman of strength

River Park Activity Day, 1977

and conviction, she taught clothing, horticulture, bicycle safety, and public speaking projects. "I am dedicated to 4-H because I know firsthand what it has to offer our children," Leon said.

In 1991, the Extension Service moved into its own building at 14700 Immokalee Road. Currently, there are two major programs: Livestock and Healthy Lifestyles. Market animal projects began in 1979 and were shown at the fair. In 2007, the First Annual Collier County 4-H Livestock Show was held in Immokalee, emphasizing livestock education and good old-fashioned family fun. There were 11 steer, 14 swine, 11 goats, 32 rabbits, 29 poultry, and 2 cavy entered. The Healthy Lifestyles Program is a partnership with Collier County Parks and Recreation. Approximately twenty children meet weekly to learn bicycling, swimming, running, and healthy eating. Many have competed in their first duathlon and look forward to finishing a triathlon.

Collier County looks forward to the next one hundred years!

61

COLUMBIA COUNTY
BY: CINDY HIGGINS

Columbia County, named for Christopher Columbus, was created in 1832. With the reconstruction of the railroad lines, Lake City became a tourist hotspot. This sparked interest due to health and vacation opportunities, coupled with the convenience of travel by train.

The University of Florida was first housed in Lake City, Columbia County, in 1883. In 1905, Henry H. Buckman, chairman of the Florida House Judiciary Committee, drafted a bill to combine the three Florida schools into three universities—what are known today as the University of Florida (UF), Florida State, and Florida A&M universities. The Buckman Act passed in May 1905, and Gainesville and Lake City were the top cities competing for UF. Lake City already housed the university and thought that it didn't have to market itself. Gainesville, however, formed

Columbia County girls give a team demonstration at the State Fair, Tampa, Florida.

Area Dairy Show, 1969. Columbia County wins High Scoring Group. From left to right are: L. Durea, Neil Dukes, Dennis Bozzuto, Richard Jones, Lauri Bozzuto, Jimmy Morgan, and John Nicely. (Paul Roy photograph)

62

a committee to promote the city. It offered $70,000 cash, agreed to pave what is now called University Avenue, and promised to provide low-cost housing for students until dorms could be built and to provide free water to the campus. On July 6, 1905, Gainesville won the bid with a 6-to-4 State Board of Control vote and the University of Florida was relocated to Gainesville, Florida.

Columbia County 4-H archives can trace pictures back about sixty years. Many of the documents were misplaced when the Extension Office moved from the courthouse to the fairgrounds in the late 1960s. Mr. Neil Dukes, the County Extension director, was instrumental in building the Columbia County Fair into what it is today.

In 2008, there were approximately 400 traditional 4-H club members that participated in twelve community clubs and 2,500 school enrichment participants. Cindy Higgins has served as the Columbia County 4-H coordinator since 1986.

DeSOTO COUNTY
BY: CHERIE HOLLINGSWORTH

As early as 1911, the Extension Program has been alive in DeSoto County. Just imagine families learning about early agriculture at this time in history. Where better to attend to their early agricultural educational needs for better ways to cultivate fields, take care of livestock, plant gardens, and preserve their foods than at the "Red Bug College" schoolhouse (one of the first elementary schools in DeSoto County, located in the Joshua Creek Community) (Melton). It is believed that the early Extension agents traveled to community gatherings and later made home or farm visits teaching the adults. Parents shared this information of better and newer ways to enrich their everyday lives with their children as many of them worked side by side on the family farm. The basic fundamentals are still alive today in DeSoto County. Here, 4-H is filled with pride in the program and the dedication of the youth and community volunteers. The wealth of information has definitely advanced the program.

As early as 1963, I had an exciting and colorful dialog with Mrs. Junia Hollingsworth not only about how the land was cleared to make the family groves and pastures, but also about how Miss Dawsey (home economics agent in 1918) would work with the girls on home economics projects such as sewing. Mrs. Hollingsworth told about going to the short course in Gainesville and how she learned many new procedures, plus had an enjoyable time socializing with others from around the state. Little did I imagine that these early activities by agents would evolve into our present-day 4-H (Hollingsworth).

Generation after generation exhibiting at the fair has been the vehicle for adults and youth to proudly show what they have produced. Since the mid-1900s, DeSoto County bonded together to proudly exhibit the best of the county. Mrs. Anne J. Campbell, home demonstration agent, said, "During the war, the State Fair booth one year was draped in the national colors and was in the shape of a hangar. The airplane was loaded with fruits and vegetables and the other articles were grouped around it" (Campbell).

Of course, in those times, the fairs were extremely important and many participated in them. You could

63

sense the heritage passing from one generation to the next. Through the 1980s, each community in DeSoto County had their own booth at the county fair. These booths shone with homegrown vegetables and fruit and also the wares that the ladies turned out.

Later on, the youth began to bring their projects to the fair to exhibit. Theresa Wheeler remembers that the boys and girls in the 1960s were part of a newly formed Pine Level 4-H community club. This club had varied 4-H projects. Ed Russell and Kenneth Sanders, Extension agents representing the Extension Service, made home visits to advise them on their beef livestock projects. "My brother, sister, and I then went on to exhibit the animals at the Tampa Fair, Ocala Fair, South West Florida Fair, and the DeSoto County Fair" (Wheeler).

The livestock area has gone from exhibiting in an open shed and less than twenty individual gated stalls to a large modern barn built in 1983. Today, the DeSoto County Fair has youth exhibiting goats,

pigs, beef animals, rabbits, and poultry. These youths are empowered by 4-H or FFA training in an organized club. The 4-H club has a Beef Livestock Club, Swine Club, Rabbit Club, Poultry Club, and Goat Club, which have bona fide requirements that help to ensure that the youth obtain the necessary education in their program before they exhibit the projects at the fair.

In early 1990, a new Exhibit Building housed the 4-H Exhibit Booth. Proudly, we have exhibited all of the projects that the members have made to complement their specific project, not to mention the "arts and crafts." Ribbons are awarded by some of our past 4-H leaders from as early as the '70s.

We can only brag about our 4-H leaders and supporters from over the years. They are always there for us. Not only as judges, passing out ribbons, but helping to organize events and major fundraisers for the program. Mary Clark traveled to Gainesville on two separate occasions to help

64

Joshua Creek School, 1913–1914. Students learn about different projects from Extension Agent Ruth Conibear. (Picture provided by Howard Melton)

Pine Level 4-H Club participates in the Arcadia All-Florida Rodeo Parade, 1960s. (Picture provided by Theresa Hollingsworth Wheeler)

the state office judge state record books. They are always ready and willing to support the program in any way they can.

The Extension and 4-H supporters have been the best! In 1983, two scholarships to four-year 4-H members have evolved. In memory of Mrs. Susie Brewer and Mrs. Mary Rutter, longtime 4-H leaders and supporters, there are two college scholarships provided. The Mary Rutter Scholarship serves the vocational interests of our members and the Susie Brewer Scholarship is for those seeking a four-year degree. Cary Mercer, a local businessman and agriculturalist, has spearheaded the Susie Brewer Scholarship to raise approximately $6,000 a year for the last twenty-five years.

As was stated earlier, the program has evolved from school and home visits to full-time clubs with volunteer adult leaders. From 1967 to 1978, Mary Ann Roe, home economics agent, worked with the youth in the schools, holding club meetings and activities at the Extension Service Office (on the second floor of the historic Eaton Building in

downtown Arcadia). One of the early groups she started was the Pine Level 4-H Club.

It is only fitting that the longest-running 4-H club for DeSoto County was first started in a history-rich area of DeSoto County. Back in 1887, the community of Pine Level was the county seat for seven counties. The "Old Pine Level" had a courthouse, post office, jail, school, two churches, and various businesses (Melton). In the mid- to late 1960s, a 4-H club was formed and met at the Pine Level Community Center. Today, you can see the markers denoting the history of this now sleepy area. Although the club changed names and volunteer leaders, this club was in existence in the same general area from 1968 to 2000. The early clubs in DeSoto County were community clubs (serving a group of youth in one area and varied project interests).

One of the first project clubs was the Arcadia 4-H Livestock Club. Diane Mullins said, "As the livestock projects grew in our larger community, the Arcadia 4-H Livestock Club was formed. This

DeSoto County 4-H School Enrichment Program, 1995. Students at Memorial Elementary School used gallon-sized plastic jugs to make masks. Pictured are Tycee Prevatt and students from Ms. Bataeman's first grade class. (Picture provided by Cherie Hollingsworth)

club was devoted to livestock and especially beef projects" (Mullins). Diane and Terry Mullins and Jim Selph, county agent, set the standards for our livestock show at the DeSoto County Fair. It didn't take long for members of this club to take top honors at other area livestock shows.

In 1979, Mr. James Selph came to DeSoto County as the Extension director and was also the director of the 4-H program. The 4-H program took great leaps to become a formal program to benefit the youth of the county. In the first year, the county went from two clubs to fourteen clubs. Not only did he build the Youth Livestock Program, but he also started an organization with the leaders: "the 4-H Leaders Forum." These meetings became the heartbeat of the DeSoto County Program and ever since have spearheaded DeSoto County 4-H to reach the magnitude it has today. We are extremely fortunate to have had a man like Mr. Selph involved in the program for over twenty-eight years with his leadership and vision.

Cindy Holly was hired in 1986 as the first full-time 4-H agent. Cindy brought to us an extensive livestock background. She exhibited a lot of energy and continued the enhancement of an ever-growing program. She was truly there for every child.

To complement the 4-H program, home economic agents, later known as food and consumer science agents, were always there to assist with the programming. Janet Drake, home economics agent from 1981 to 1999, was well known for her 4-H involvement and her "bread-in-the-bag" and other nutritious programs in the public schools. Pam Phillipee, home economics agent from 1999 to 2000, is remembered for her assistance with programming at the City of Arcadia Parks and Recreation summer programs. From 2001 to 2005, Susan Rachles, food and consumer science agent, took the lead for presenting healthy eating programs.

In 1990, Karyn Gary became our 4-H agent, and she introduced the Century 21 and 4-H after-school programming, including new state in-school enrichment programs. The youth enjoyed the programs such as: recycling with accompanied arts and crafts masks, the Holiday Planter, and embryology (chick hatching) to name a few. These programs are still going strong.

Tycee Prevatt, 4-H agent from 1993 to 1995, had a great understanding of the senior 4-H programs. With Tycee's roots to Manatee County, she started our involvement in the 4-H Tropicana Speech Contest.

In 2001, Christa Carlson became our 4-H agent. Christa served as 4-H agent for five years, which included the time period that Hurricane Charlie blew through DeSoto County. Two days after the devastation of the hurricane, Jim Selph, the County Extension director, designated our office as the agricultural distress center. Christa was extremely helpful during this period because of her excellent leadership and organizational abilities.

Today, we are housed in a terrific facility. Our new building was constructed and we moved into the facility in 2002.

Christi Pryor came on board in February of 2007 as the 4-H agent. In her first year, 4-H saw an increase in membership of approximately 50 percent and a number of new clubs have been added. Christi has lots of enthusiasm and energy and even greater 4-H happenings are on the horizon for DeSoto County.

The DeSoto County 4-H Junior Cattlemen Club members participate in the Beef Quiz Bowl, 2007. From left to right, back row: Christi Candelora, Phil Turner, Jim Selph, Jimmy Fussell, and Joyce Hunter. Front row: Niki Emery, Kayla Patton, Christi Pryor, Paige Hamrick, and Whitney Walker.

DeSoto County 4-H'ers attend the National 4-H 100-Year celebration parade in St. Augustine, Florida, 2002. From left to right are Jessica Young, Cherie Hollingsworth, Robin Hastings, and Eli Dyal. (Picture provided by DeSoto County 4-H)

DIXIE COUNTY

The Dixie County 4-H Program remains rural, and food and nutrition projects were the most popular as of 2007. In 2007, there were 1,524 members enrolled in 1,822 projects. There were sixty-three 4-H clubs and seventy-four adult volunteers.

State Boys' 4-H Council, 1958–1959, Tampa, Florida. From left to right, standing, are district representatives Larry Bowers, DeFuniak Springs; Johnny Yaun, Moore Haven; Max Beebe, West Palm Beach; Harold Chapman, St. Augustine; Alvin Henderson, Lee; and Jack Boyd, Brooksville. Seated: Don Hanson, Marianna, reporter; Bill Nelson, Melbourne, treasurer; Paul Hendrick, Jasper, secretary; Herman Somers, Gainesville, vice-president; and Tom Peter Chaires III, Old Town, president.

DUVAL COUNTY
BY: JUDIE TOULOUSE AND LESLIE ALLEN

The 4-H club was established in 1915 in Duval County. Corn clubs, formed by W. L. Watson, Extension agent from 1914 to 1927, targeted boys. The girls' tomato clubs addressed the home economics area. In 1917, Duval 4-H hosted the first State Poultry Show. During World War I, 4-H club projects targeted the war effort.

Over the years, participation at the fair has proven to be a vital part of the county 4-H program. In 1932, ten 4-H boys paraded their "thoroughbred" calves through downtown Jacksonville (*The Florida Times Union*, February 2, 1932).

During World War II, 4-H Victory Gardens were found in city parks and near apartments. "Learn by doing" bonded the city and rural members. Community service projects during wartime consisted of salvage collecting, saving scrap metal and fats, conserving machinery, and clothing and foods. New projects evolved to meet the needs of our youth. In 1945, one hundred leaders of twenty-four 4-H clubs honored members for their club work. Agents Mildred Taylor and Gordon B. Ellis were in charge.

In the 1960s, Duval County established a 4-H Advisory Committee to give guidance to the 4-H program and to sponsor committees for 4-H clubs to extend support for volunteers. Previously, 4-H clubs were conducted in the schools. In 1965, 4-H community clubs became integrated organized clubs. Since then, 4-H club leadership has been provided by volunteers trained by the county agent. Tom Braddock, an agent from 1957 to 1995, provided leadership. The 4-H club in Duval County was instrumental in accepting the concept of integration. A 4-H volunteer standing on the dock at Camp Cherry Lake told about the great feeling of seeing youth of different races able to "learn by doing" and break down the barriers that were so prevalent at the time. Wilma Tindell volunteered thirty years of service to 4-H. In 1969, there were 500 youth in twenty-six community clubs.

The Duval County 4-H Foundation was established in 1973. A membership campaign began in 1984 for funds to enhance programs and initiate new innovative ones. An endowment fund was established in 1999 so that funds wouldn't be affected by the economy. Private funds that are available for 4-H programs have increased to over $200,000.

Public Speaking, 1959. From left to right are Donna Frazee, Rex Brown, and Nellie Weaver.

In the 1980s, oceanic and space exploration unfolded for 4-H'ers through the Sea Grant Extension and Blue Sky projects. Marilyn Halusky was 4-H program leader from 1976 to 1998. Although agriculture projects remained, as rural land diminished, emphasis shifted to more urban content. To supplement Florida training in the district, specialists from Ohio, Pennsylvania, Iowa, and New York were brought to Jacksonville using 4-H Foundation funds to train volunteers. Marge Modesky has volunteered for thirty years and was instrumental in starting "My Government Day," which is still a current program.

To learn more about different cultures, an International and National 4-H Exchange Program was formed in 1986. By living with host families, teens develop a keener appreciation of values and culture. The Exchange Club is our longest continuous 4-H club. Leslie Allen has been a volunteer for thirty years and is the current advisor.

69

Arlington 4-H boys and girls, 1943

In the 1990s, over 22,000 4-H youth per year were in 4-H through eighty-six community clubs, the Expanded Food and Nutrition Education Program, and school enrichment programs. With an emphasis on leadership, citizenship, marine science, horticulture, food and nutrition, and new technology including rocketry and computers, 4-H stayed relevant as the dynamics of urban Jacksonville changed. Programs such as the "I Can, We Can" Challenge Adventure were popular with teens. "Expedition Training" enabled teens to make their own decisions in an outdoor environment and to accept the consequences. Asset building was introduced to evaluate the impact of 4-H club work on life skills. Over the years, agriculture projects grew to include more urban-style projects.

Camping has always been an essential part of the 4-H program. Residential and day camps are held throughout the summer. The emphasis of 4-H Camp Cherry Lake is on conservation and ecology, building basic life skills, and developing friendships.

Delores Kesler, founder of Kesler Mentoring Connection, a multi-billion-dollar business, stated, "without the mentoring I received from 4-H, I would have been a very different person today. 4-H had a tremendous impact on my leadership aspirations. I will always owe a debt to the wonderful 4-H staff and volunteers who spent their time and energy developing a kid who grew up on a farm in Dinsmore."

71

ESCAMBIA COUNTY
BY: LATESSA ESTES

Escambia County is very proud of its rich 4-H history. Barrineau Park 4-H Club was the first, organized in 1914. Several of the clubs in Escambia County have been passed down through family generations. The 4-H program has enabled numerous young people to develop many skills and become productive citizens. Over the years, there has always been a strong effort to adapt and change programs to best suit the needs of the 4-H youth.

Volunteers have always been a vital part of Escambia County 4-H, and without them, the program would not be where it is today. Programs and projects can only be as good as the people implementing them, and Escambia County has been blessed with wonderful agents that have gone above and beyond their call of duty for the greater good of our 4-H youth. The first agents in Escambia County were Ed Finelayson and Ethel Atkinson. Since then, there have been many agents that have led programs and we thank them all.

In the 1920s and 1930s, 4-H projects consisted of corn clubs, livestock, tomato clubs, sewing, and gardening. During that period, girls and boys had separate clubs.

The 1940s started with all efforts directed toward World War II, and the slogan "Food for Freedom" was adopted. The 4-H youth helped take care of livestock for Escambia County soldiers during World War II. The '40s also hold a very special place in Escambia County 4-H history; a much-respected man saw the need for 4-H youth to have a local place to call their own. Langley Bell sold 400 acres to Escambia County 4-H clubs for the total cost of $1. The landscape, buildings,

Here, 4-H'ers practice fishing techniques with the help of a volunteer.

and directions of the Langley Bell Center have changed over the last sixty-five years, but the love of the property and deep heritage have survived many adversities. Some of the property was sold to make way for an interstate and other development. Funds from the sale were invested to provide stability for the Langley Bell Center and Escambia County 4-H. To commemorate his dedication, a special Langley Bell ring is awarded to the top two 4-H youth each year. The Langley

Bell Center holds special memories for many in Escambia County because it gave them a local place to camp, fish, and explore new projects.

The 1950s brought change and excitement with the new national effort concentrating on citizenship and a special interest in science. Escambia County's livestock judging team from Pineforest 4-H Club won at state and continued to win second place in the nation.

In the 1960s, the first ethnic clubs were formed in Escambia County, and two generations later are still very active in the Olive Heights 4-H Club. On a national level, minorities were encouraged to participate in national 4-H events and expanded 4-H to serve disadvantaged youth in both rural and urban areas.

The 1970s came with new interest groups and 4-H continued to change and grow with more of an effort to publicize 4-H. Volunteers were able to take a more active role, and were able to enrich the lives of youth in Escambia County. The Diamond N 4-H Club formed the first horse judging team and was sponsored by the Pensacola Interstate Fair to travel to Louisville, Kentucky, to compete in the national judging contest.

Escambia County started the 4-H Chautauqua in the '80s and was able to raise funds to further all 4-H projects. Twenty years later, the excitement can still be heard in the voices of those who participated.

The '90s brought expansion with the Tropicana Public Speaking enrichment program in Escambia County. At the time of this writing, over 30,000 youth have participated in Escambia County.

In the years 2000 to 2008, Escambia County is especially proud of the way it has transformed through the years to meet the needs of its 4-H

Volunteers play an important role in teaching youth about projects.

Members, alumni, volunteers, and faculty of 4-H celebrate Florida 4-H, 2007. (Courtesy of Tess Estes)

youth. Through many adversities and budget cuts, the staff, volunteers, and youth have found that combined, they can make a difference. The trials have only made the spirit of past and present 4-H'ers come alive to fight for the future of 4-H. As 4-H'ers young and old reflect on their accomplishments, they realize what an important part 4-H has played in their lives. They want to protect that for the future.

FLAGLER COUNTY
BY: SUSAN LOVELACE

Flagler County made its first announcement about the 4-H Youth Program in the October 28, 1926 edition of the local newspaper, the *Flagler Tribune*. In the monthly county agents' column, it was written that "farm boys and girls of Flagler County would soon organize 4-H clubs as a way to make the most of their opportunities for a life of greater usefulness and achievement." The article referred to 4-H as the "Florida State Organization of Agricultural Clubs." Boys dominated the early agricultural clubs and learned about various lines of farm work, including raising pigs, cattle, chickens, or growing an acre of corn or potatoes. The 4-H clubs were often referred to as the local agricultural clubs and 4-H boys' clubs. The article emphasized that merely growing an acre of corn or raising a flock of chickens will give a club member a better chance for success in life. But rather it is the spirit in which this work is done and the training that goes into it that helps develop independence, confidence, self-reliance, and a love of farm work.

The first three 4-H clubs consisted of thirty-four members in Flagler County and were organized by Agricultural Agent L. T. Nielsen in 1926. The boys and girls enrolled from three area schools: Bunnell High School, Haw Creek School, and Gilbert School. The clubs of this time were the St. Johns Park 4-H Club, the 4-H Poultry Club, and the 4-H Forestry Club. "The Flagler County 4-H Forestry Club has the distinction of being the first of its kind" (Holland, Mary). It was organized and led by Agent L. T. Nielsen. The boys in this club transplanted trees at the local school; took field trips, including a trip to the Forestry Experiment Station at Starke, Florida; and studied forestry topics such as fire protection, natural reforestation, and forest conservation.

The history of Flagler County 4-H is rich in agricultural tradition. Since its inception, the majority of 4-H members have sought out opportunities to participate in poultry, dairy and beef cattle, swine, and rabbit projects before any other project topics.

Flagler County 4-H boys and girls typically exhibited their livestock projects at the Volusia and Putnam County Fairs until Flagler established its own fair in the 1980s. Brenda Boyd, a long-time resident of Flagler County, said that in the early 1960s, young 4-H members gathered at the Civic Center behind Bunnell High School to show livestock. In 1965, 4-H held its local livestock show on the front lawn of the Flagler County Courthouse.

Flagler County was without an agricultural agent for nearly a quarter century after L. T. Neilsen left Extension to work for the Florida Forestry Service. In the late 1950s, Frank Polhill was hired as the new agricultural agent. Under the guidance of this agent and future agents, Flagler County 4-H'ers actively participated in district and state events throughout its history, including competitions in Tampa and Jacksonville and also the Central Florida Fair where youth participated and placed in the State Dairy Show in the late 1960s.

Each summer, Flagler County 4-H members attend annual camp. Records show that Flagler camped at Camp McQuarrie in the Ocala National Forest, at Camp Cherry Lake in Madison County, and today, at Camp Ocala. In addition to camp, 4-H members participated in livestock and poultry shows, which date back to the 1930s. By 1955, there were 2,000 4-H boys and girls from Duval, Nassau, Baker, Putnam, Clay, Bradford, St. Johns, and Flagler counties who would compete at events

Above: Abby Cody, a member of Haw Creek Gator Cloverbud Club in Bunnell, is shown here with her rabbit project, January 2008. (Michelle Bratcher, photographer)

Below: Jacob Boyd presents his beef cattle project at the Flagler County Fair, April 2007. (Patricia Cody, photographer)

in different classes such as poultry, eggs, dairy and beef cattle, swine, and rabbit.

Although animal science projects have always been the leading area of interest, Flagler County

4-H in its time has also offered cooking clubs, marine science clubs, camping clubs, and horse clubs.

FRANKLIN COUNTY
BY: WILLIAM MAHAN, JR.

Franklin County Extension dates back to around the mid-1950s, when Bill Zorn was the county's first agriculture agent and County Extension director.

In the 1970s, Franklin County had approximately four to six 4-H clubs. They had a very active horse club and summer camping program. The county's 4-H'ers were also very involved in county, district, state, and national events. In the late 1970s, 4-H activities in the county dropped off when the county's Home Economics/4-H Agent Ms. Toni Taranto accepted a home economics teaching position at Apalachicola High School. Her position was advertised several times in an effort to refill the position; however, the university was unable to find a replacement for the position, and over time the position was lost, leaving one agent/County Extension director position in the county.

When Jim Estes retired as the county's agriculture/ County Extension director in 1989, the Extension Office was closed until June 1993, when Bill Mahan, Jr. was hired as the new Sea Grant agent/ County Extension director.

During Mahan's first year, the 4-H program had approximately thirty 4-H'ers participate in a 4-H school enrichment program on car seat and seat belt safety, which was sponsored by the Florida Department of Transportation (FDOT). In the second program year, a Marine Science 4-H Club was formed by six high-school-aged students with the goal of competing in the State 4-H Marine

Ecology Judging Event held at Camp Ocala. In addition, approximately 300 4-H'ers participated in the FDOT-sponsored 4-H Car Seat and Seat Belt Safety Program, and approximately sixty 4-H'ers in fourth, fifth, and sixth grade participated in the 4-H Tropicana Public Speaking Program.

Since the 1994–1995 program year, several 4-H programs and clubs have come and gone. In 1996, the Marine 4-H Club disbanded, saying that getting ready to compete in the State Judging Event was too much like school. However, many of the same 4-H'ers then formed a 4-H Sailing Club that was sponsored by the Apalachicola Maritime Museum, the home of the *Governor Stone*, a historic sailing vessel (schooner) built in 1877, that the club members sailed. The club, however, also sailed away after one year.

In 1997, Lydia Countryman, a special education teacher at Brown Elementary School, formed the first long-term 4-H club in recent history in Franklin County. Ms. Countryman's special education students were very active 4-H'ers for three years. During their time as a club, they were very active in community service projects throughout Franklin County. The members participated in coastal clean-ups and did fundraisers to purchase "ouch" dolls for the county's ambulance service to give to sick and injured children who needed to be transported via ambulance for medical care. The 4-H'ers also built and maintained a nature trail around the school for all the students to enjoy. The club and its members received a number of recognitions and awards during their three years in existence for their community service efforts. The club ended in 2000, when Ms. Countryman accepted a teaching job in Georgia.

Since 2000, only one additional club has formed as an after-school 4-H club at the Apalachicola Bay Charter School. The club was called ABC WINGS, formed in 2007 to study butterflies as part of Project Butterfly WINGS: Winning Investigative Network for Great Science, a 4-H program done in cooperation with the Florida Museum of Natural History.

However, the fact that 4-H clubs have come and gone over the years doesn't mean that Franklin County doesn't have an "active" 4-H program. The "regular" 4-H activities that occur in the county include:

• 4-H Tropicana Public Speaking Program – This is the longest-running 4-H program in the county and typically has about 250 4-H'ers each year. As Ms. Leanna Parrish, a teacher volunteer who has been involved with the speech competition, said last year: "It's kind of scary when you think about the 4-H Tropicana Speech Contest these days. Because we have been doing it so long, some of the original fourth-, fifth-, and sixth-graders who participated have returned to school as teachers!"

• 4-H Butterfly Development Program – This program, now in its tenth year, was developed as a 4-H school enrichment program to educate local youth about butterflies and moths living in our area. The program focuses on the annual monarch butterfly migration that flies through Franklin County each fall and watching and documenting the metamorphosis of the painted

lady butterfly as it grows as a caterpillar, pupa, and finally hatches into an adult butterfly. Students/4-H'ers in all grades participate in this program, from Pre-K through twelfth grade. In a typical year, 700 to 800 4-H'ers participate in this program. The total student enrollment for Franklin County Schools is 1,100 to 1,200 students.

• 4-H County Camp – When it comes to memories that former 4-H'ers, now adults, have about their times in 4-H, their days at 4-H Camp Timpoochee are probably the number one memory. In fact, I have had many a Franklin County "senior" (sixty years old and over) stop and tell me stories from their days at camp. Even today, camp is a popular summer activity for Franklin County 4-H'ers. With camp planning underway for this summer, a number of 4-H'ers have already told me that they are planning on going to camp again this year. Over the past few years, Franklin County has averaged fifteen campers and we have teamed up with 4-H'ers from Holmes and Walton counties in Florida as well as Covington County in Alabama for our summer camping experience.

GADSDEN COUNTY
BY: YOLANDA Y. GOODE

There are several areas one could choose to focus on during the one-hundredth-year celebration of Florida 4-H, but space is limited. This article will focus on the generational participation in Gadsden County 4-H Livestock Club.

First, here is a brief historical perspective of the Gadsden County 4-H Program, which has been in existence over eighty years. This program began during segregation. There were separate clubs for African-American and white youth as well as gender-specific clubs. Extension staff from Florida A&M University and the University of Florida Cooperative Extension serviced the clientele respectively. The main project areas back then were home economics and agriculture.

Fast-forwarding to the present, there are no longer gender- or race-specific clubs. In the livestock project area, the number of male and female participants are about equal. Gadsden County

4-H has also expanded its programming to include science and technology and shooting sports.

The Gadsden County 4-H Livestock Club has provided youth the opportunity to develop lifelong skills while learning to care for, exhibit, and judge livestock for six decades. There are only a few families who have the honor of having three generations participate in the Gadsden 4-H Livestock Club. Only two families will be featured in this article, but the Dwight Clark family needs to be mentioned.

Angel Clark Granger

Nelson Clark, the father of the retired Gadsden County 4-H Livestock Club Leader Angel Clark Granger, showed in the 1950s. Angel followed in her father's footsteps in the 1970s, and her sons Cole and Cody Granger participated in the mid-'90s through 2006. Their family had the first third-generational exhibitors in the West Florida Livestock Show and Sale.

78

Nelson Clark

When asked how her family has benefited from participating in the Gadsden County 4-H Livestock Club, Angel Clark Granger had this to say: "4-H gave them a sense of family and a greater appreciation of the importance of agriculture. 4-H keeps families together, closer, and working together. 4-H teaches children responsibility and gives them a better edge in life."

Ethan and Eltan "Jake" Moore followed in their father's—Gerard Moore (1970s)—and grandfather's—Herman Moore (1950s)—footsteps by participating in the Gadsden County 4-H Livestock Club.

Gerard echoed some of the same sentiments that Angel did when asked how his family has benefited from participating in the Gadsden County 4-H

Livestock Club. He stated: "Participation in the Gadsden County 4-H Program help them meet other families, develop social skills, and created an opportunity to see the legacy of participation in his family and others."

It is great to know that Gadsden County 4-H Livestock Club has played an integral part in developing young people for at least six decades. One has to acknowledge that in other 4-H program areas, there is multi-generational family participation. The thought from Gerard Moore that families can actually create their own legacy through 4-H is an amazing idea. Gadsden County 4-H is rooted in its rich history but is ever adapting to provide all youth the opportunity to make the best better.

GILCHRIST COUNTY
BY: CHRIS DeCUBELLIS

Gilchrist County is rural with traditional culture and an agriculture-based economy. Dairy and beef cattle enterprises, watermelons, and agronomic crops make up the bulk of agriculture in the county. Traditionally Trenton, Bell, and Fanning Springs are the main towns in the county. The 4-H program currently consists of eighteen traditional community clubs that serve approximately 275 youth club members along with a school enrichment program that consists of an embryology project that serves every third-grader in the county. The Gilchrist County Program is rich in traditional 4-H projects like vegetable gardening, livestock projects, and shooting sports. In everything we do, we stress the importance of the cornerstones of 4-H youth development: citizenship, leadership, communication skills, and through success in these areas, an enhancement of self-esteem.

Poultry Judging Contest

Cole Deipersloot with his garden project

GLADES COUNTY
BY: COURTNEY DAVIS

"Where Sugar Comes From," demonstration by David Kilpatrick, May 2003

Glades County 4-H Program officially started in September 1959. Agricultural Agent Billy O. Bass was the first 4-H agent in Glades County. There were two clubs and a total membership of fifty-five. In their first year, Glades County 4-H participated in the Southwest Florida Fair with eight head of livestock, one entry in the tractor-driving contest, and two livestock judging teams. They also went to Camp Cloverleaf for a swimming party and a

Glades County campers canoeing. Camp Cloverleaf, 2004.

"wiener roast." With the start of a 4-H program, they also started the first youth livestock fair, where they had eighteen youth participate. The first two 4-H leaders were Mrs. Juanell Peeples and Mrs. Katheryn Bronson.

In 1964, the Doyle Conner Agricultural Center was built in Glades County. The agricultural Extension agent is housed at this facility.

For many years, Secretary Patricia Stroud of the Extension Office maintained the 4-H program in Glades County. She was employed from 1970 to 2005. She is still an avid supporter of the 4-H program.

Glades County 4-H still has many of the same programs that it started with less than fifty years ago. Every year, more than one hundred members of 4-H show in what is now called the Glades Youth Livestock

Glades County youth livestock show, 2003

Show, held in conjunction with the Chalo Nitka festival. Chalo Nitka means "Big Bass" in Seminole. Many of the members also travel to the South Florida Fair, Central Florida Fair, and the Florida State Fair to show their animals. The 4-H club still takes many students to Camp Cloverleaf for the annual summer camp.

In the 2007–2008 year, we have 109 members. Glades 4-H has a dairy club, "Cows-R-Us"; two steer clubs, "Beefmakers" and "Drag and Lead"; one swine club, "Rooters"; and a cloverbud club called the "Little Rascals." The "Little Rascals" are able to show baby livestock animals in the fair, a long-standing tradition that is very endearing for the Glades County community. These clubs participate in the livestock fair year after year.

Dusty Wilson and Amy Lundy showing dairy cattle.
South Florida Fair, February 1, 2008.

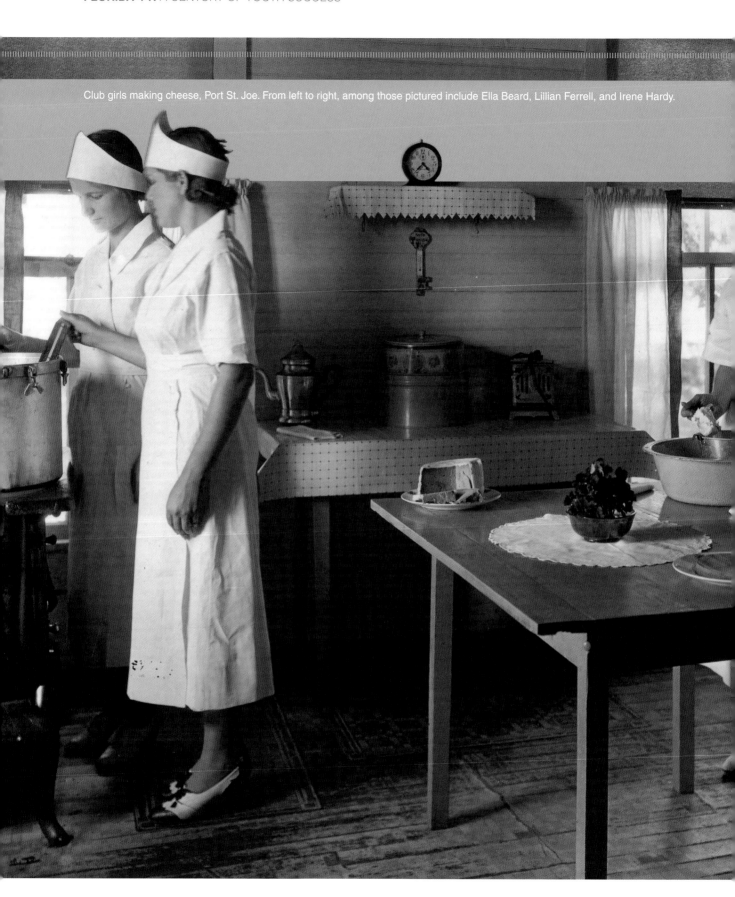

Club girls making cheese, Port St. Joe. From left to right, among those pictured include Ella Beard, Lillian Ferrell, and Irene Hardy.

GULF COUNTY

Since the 1940s, agriculture and 4-H were major programs in Gulf County. The major projects that 4-H'ers partake in currently are horses, horticulture, fish pond management, school gardens, agriculture, and 4-H Camp Timpoochee. For the past five years, Roy Carter, the County Extension director, has helped deliver Agriculture Exploration Days, ag-awareness days at locations around the county.

For the past twenty years, the Gulf County 4-H club "Big River Riders" has been in existence. The club is currently led by Jean McMillian with the help of Julie Wester. This club focuses on the 4-H Horse Project, where 4-H'ers participate in horse shows and Horse Quiz Bowl contests. The members of this club also participate in leadership events. Another notable event that has taken place in Gulf County for the past twenty years is the Tupelo Honey Festival. This festival is a fundraiser and also recognizes the biggest agricultural industry in the area: Tupelo Honey.

83

HAMILTON COUNTY
BY: HEATHER FUTCH

Provisions were made for agricultural Extension programs for the State of Florida in 1919, with one program to be headquartered in Live Oak, Florida. Milharg was the first recorded employee for this program. Secrist was another early agent serving the area. S. S. Smith was employed in 1915 as a cooperative demonstration agent, and had corn and tomato clubs (Lewis, M. D., et al.). Many members of the community became heavily involved as leaders for the youth clubs and many youth became members. Originally the Extension staff was housed in the local post office (Tyree, A. B. 2007). County governments found that these buildings had enough additional space to house a few extra offices and was perfect for Extension staff. This lasted until the late 1960s or early 1970s.

84

Promoting 4-H at local parades is popular around the state.

Nesmith was employed as county agent in 1941 and after he retired, in 1954, Rance Andrews was employed as County Extension director to begin the more modern era of 4-H in the county (Lewis, M. D., et al.). As a previous member of 4-H, Andrews brought hog, dairy, poultry, and corn yield contests into Hamilton County. As more people became involved in these events and more

events were added, the day these activities were held was eventually established as Events Day in 1971 (Tyree, A. B. 2007). County Events Day, which was the equivalent of a fair day, included a pig scramble, dairy cattle show, barrow show and sale, and a horse show (*Jasper News*, 1956–1971). Later, it was changed to a multitude of days, and then changed again back to its present-day form of one day (Tyree, A. B. 2007). Andrews was the founder of the Hamilton County Fair Association and worked to obtain fairgrounds for Events Day. He was successful in securing land for both the fairgrounds and an arena for the horse club (Tyree, A. B. 2007).

A 4-H girl with her swine project.

The first Hamilton County Extension home demonstration agent was Wylma White, employed in 1955. Ms. White held responsibility for working with white female 4-H'ers. Although in 1940 the beginning of the girls' clubs in Hamilton County were recorded, White is credited with beginning the first organized clubs. She began numerous home demonstration clubs, Fashion Revues, and girls' short courses throughout the county. She

County Dairy Show winners, 1961

compiled a weekly article for the *Jasper News*, which discussed the home and garden, and also kept the community up-to-date with regular announcements about 4-H in the newspaper. She kept a scrapbook of these clippings which still exists in the Hamilton County Extension Office (Tyree, A. B. 2007).

Noah Bennett, the first county agent of African-American descent, was employed in 1939. Isaac Chandler began in 1953 and continued to serve until 1988 (Lewis, M. D., et al.). Due to segregation at the time, Chandler, an African-American, was housed in a separate office and was even required to chop his own wood for his office wood-burning heater (Tyree, A. B. 2007). Chandler began his career by organizing school and community clubs for African-American boys and working on corn

and swine projects. After integration, Chandler received the majority of the responsibility for the 4-H program in Hamilton County (Tyree, A. B. 2007). Ms. White continued to put a great deal of work into the program throughout her tenure as an Extension agent in Hamilton County.

In 1955, clubs in the county started having monthly socials at their club meetings, and by 1957, they were having a yearly social gathering of all clubs (*Jasper News*, 1956–1971). Originally there were three clubs, one in each elementary school in the county. This evolved in 1957 with the creation of the Midway 4-H Community Club, which was sponsored by the Midway Home Demonstration Club (also led by Wylma White). Other community clubs continued to form, including White Springs, New Hope, Jennings, Jasper, and Marion Station community clubs (*Jasper News*, 1956–1971). White led the groups to begin a county council in 1957 and then trained them to plan the program for the year. There was also a County Song Group, which later became the 4-H Choir. Classes like Beginning Sewing, Branch Weaving, and Apron Making were held, and clubs held car washes, fashion shows, and quilt shows to raise money (*Jasper News*, 1956–1971).

The 4-H clubs maintained the landscaping around the county courthouse (Tyree, A. B. 2007). Many members competed in a broad array of contests, including forest ecology, horticulture, cherry pie-making, dairy foods, talent contests, public speaking, and lamp-making. Their projects ranged from crafts, copper models, and candles, to corn, silage, livestock, and hay. The 4-H program held a County Demonstration Day yearly in which youth would give talks about their project area and then compete for an opportunity to present at the District Demonstration Day (*Jasper News*, 1956–1971). Each year, a 4-H banquet was held to honor members of the clubs in the county.

The 4-H club lost its vigor once the schools in the county consolidated (Tyree, A. B. 2007). Previously, in each of the three major towns in the county— Jasper, Jennings, and White Springs—there had been an elementary, middle, and high school. However, in 1968, the schools were consolidated into three schools and centralized in Jasper. The 4-H program lost the community support it had once seen.

In 1988, there were twenty-two active volunteers, four 4-H units, and fifty-five total youth being reached. In 2006, there were ninety-eight active volunteers, thirty-five 4-H units, and 1,173 total youth being reached. Traditionally, the 4-H program in Hamilton County has been school-

based. This is the way it was in 1988, when Greg Hicks inherited the program as agriculture/4-H agent. The program has continued that way until 2007, when Heather Futch was hired as 4-H/family and consumer sciences agent. As of 2007, there were two community clubs in the Hamilton

Campers at Camp Cherry Lake learn new things each year.

County 4-H Program. However, school enrichment continues in Hamilton County. Teachers use Extension-developed curriculum with students in their classrooms.

Seatbelt Safety was a big program in Hamilton County from 1990 to 2006. One of the activities in this program was the Seatbelt Safety Poster Contest. Since 1990, Hamilton County has had eight youth who have placed in the top three in their respective categories in the Florida state competition. The county has also had two youth with honorable mentions in the contest.

Other activities currently in Hamilton County include embryology in the classroom, livestock and farm judging, Youth Ag Day, Farm and Home Safety Day, plant propagation, and County Fair Day with livestock projects. Also, there is a yearly Earth Day celebration, a Natural Resources Day Camp, a Water Quality Day Camp, and residential 4-H summer camp.

HARDEE COUNTY
BY: SANDY SCOTT

The early days of Hardee County found its citizens taking advantage of the richness of the soil, and they soon discovered that the fields would produce an abundance of strawberries, cucumbers, potatoes, corn, and tomatoes. Livestock dotted the vast acreage of land where cattle grazed and were eventually taken to the local market.

Wives were busy canning vegetables retrieved from their personal gardens and young girls learned quickly the expertise of "putting up" jams and jellies from the fruits harvested from strawberry plants, pear and kumquat trees, and grape arbors. The art of embroidering, sewing, and quilting was taught to young Hardee County girls by their mothers, grandmothers, and great-grandmothers. Soon, an entity emerged in which these youngsters could participate.

Hardee County 4-H clubs have been important since the 1930s, when students could participate in their local neighborhoods of Wauchula, Bowling Green, Zolfo Springs, Gardner, Ona, Limestone, and many others that would soon disappear.

The war years of the 1940s saw other activities in which 4-H members were involved. Headlines of food rationing, the collection of rubber, and liberty gardens made their way to Hardee County, and these clubs contributed much to the war effort.

As this county was emerging into a prosperous and growing community, so was the 4-H organization. In the 1950s, young girls learned the art of homemaking skills, including sewing, embroidery, and table-setting. Boys learned how to care for cattle and swine, and other projects included photography, gardening, and leadership.

Club meetings were held on the school grounds in the early years, and the Hardee County school system has always been a proponent of the 4-H organization. Members of 4-H clubs were photographed as a group and they were included in the yearbook along with other school clubs.

Margie and Kathy Hodges do a demonstration at the Tampa State Fair, 1953.

Hardee County was still rich in the soil that made its way into the prominence of this agricultural community. Projects including cattle, swine, chickens, and rabbits flowed over to the female 4-H'ers as years passed.

These clubs have been important to the children and the community has always been a strong supporter of the 4-H organization. Over the years, the types of clubs available for students to join has increased to include those of gardening, poultry, sewing, culinary arts, sport fishing, and shooting sports, as well as the traditional swine, steer, and dairy clubs.

Camp Ocala, summer of 1952

During the third week of February, students are able to show off their skills at the Hardee County Fair. Their animals are transported to the fair grounds and each 4-H member is responsible for the total care of his or her project. This care begins prior to the beginning of the school day, continues after school is out, and on into the evening hours during this weeklong event. During those hours, the animals are fed, groomed, and prepared for the actual showing within the arena. The stalls are kept clean by constantly raking the area. It is not unusual to catch a glimpse of a student climbing over the fence which holds his or her prize pig and replenishing the container with water. The highlight of the week's fair events includes the judging and issuance of the ribbons that the students receive for their hard work.

Of the eleven active clubs in Hardee County, the longest-running club is "Country Clovers." They are a special interest club whose primary focus is that of raising swine, poultry, and rabbits. The majority of these members raise swine.

Membership has remained steady throughout the years. In August, an open house is held and each club is represented. Here, new prospective members may talk to leaders and obtain miscellaneous information concerning the projects associated with that particular club. It is here that many new members are able to choose just the right club that sparks his or her interest.

Many Hardee County 4-H Club members progressed in their endeavors and participated on County Council as well as at the state level. Those early years of 4-H have produced teachers, principals, state legislators, and county administrators. These individuals are quick to agree that the lessons they learned were invaluable. They learned how to make the best better and to take constructive criticism. Their lives have been impacted by the 4-H organization and they have passed on the importance of this program for the generations of children who have followed after them.

Distinguished alumni from Hardee County include Earl Ray Gill, who was inducted into the Florida 4-H Alumni Hall of Fame in 2006. Ruth Carsten Hodges was a member of the Florida State Silver-Haired Legislature and had been a volunteer 4-H leader and prominent educator for over two decades.

When former 4-H members have an opportunity to speak at Hardee County civic clubs, each is eager to explain the influence that this organization has had on their lives. It has helped them make a way for themselves in the business world by being articulate in the art of public speaking, by being a responsible individual, and by taking an avid interest in their community. Hardee County has most assuredly reaped the rewards of the influence of the 4-H organization.

HENDRY COUNTY
BY: SONJA CRAWFORD

Hendry County lies on the southern shore of Lake Okeechobee and touches the banks of the Caloosahatchee River. It was created by an act of the Florida Legislature in 1923. The county government was formed and began its official duties on July 1, 1923. The area of Hendry County was formerly a part of Lee County, as was Collier County to the south.

According to Mr. Frank Polhill, the Hendry County 4-H Program began prior to his employment as an Extension agent in 1957. Mr. Polhill retired in 1963. The first project area known to the Hendry County 4-H Program was the cattle club led by the late Mr. Robinson, later led by the late Dr. Kenneth Keen, DVM. It is the longest-running club in the county and is currently under the leadership of Mr. and Mrs. Kenny Wayne Keen.

The development of home demonstration clubs began with the employment of Mrs. Zelma Keen in 1967. Mrs. Keen was the first 4-H program assistant known to the State of Florida. Her employment began from a University of Florida grant to work with minorities. Mrs. Keen worked with the Seminole Indians on the Big Cypress Indian Reservation in the areas of sewing and cooking.

Patricia Bosley moved to Hendry County from Ft. Lauderdale in the late 1970s. Since Pioneer Plantation was located twenty-five miles from town, there was very little the youth in the community could participate in without traveling to Clewiston or LaBelle. Therefore, she enrolled her three older children, ages ten, twelve, and fourteen, in the local community 4-H club. The leader of the 4-H club moved away after the first 4-H club meeting. Instead of the 4-H club disbanding, Mrs. Bosley

Hendry County Steer Show. From left to right are Erin Zimmerly and Josie Boykin.

Florida 4-H Meat Judging first-place team, Hendry County, July 1989. This team also won first place at the National 4-H Meat Judging Competition. From left to right are Sonja Crews, Becki Crews, and Shelley Willis.

took leadership over the 4-H club and is still a club leader in the Pioneer Community today. Mrs. Bosley gained the satisfaction of receiving the Salute to Excellence Lifetime Volunteer Award through the National 4-H Council in 2003 for her dedication to the youth of Hendry County.

Sonja Crews Crawford (left) presents the Volunteer of the Year award to Patricia Bosley (right).

Hendry County 4-H youth at the Florida State Capitol. From left to right are: James McCall, Ishmael Seymour, Adam Bechtel, Representative Spratt, Melissa Gonzalez, Wendy Kirkland, Tana Wright, and Christina Morales.

90

Today, the Hendry County 4-H Program consists of many project areas for youth to develop life skills, such as communication, citizenship, decision-making, leadership, and interpersonal relationships. By acquiring life skills, youth learn about practical problems they will face in life. Subject matter curricula help youth understand research-based educational topics and learn how to think about and solve problems. In the broadest sense, 4-H is a human development program designed to foster a sense of confidence, a feeling of accomplishment, and a heightened level of competence. The 4-H youth in Hendry County grow and learn with help from parents, leaders, interested community members, and cooperative Extension professionals.

HERNANDO COUNTY
BY: TORINA "T.C." SCHMIDT

The Hernando County 4-H Program began early in the second decade of the 1900s. It started as school-based clubs managed by the agriculture agents and home economics (FCS) agents for over the first sixty years of its existence. The focus of the clubs in these early years was primarily agriculture, livestock, horticulture, crop growing, and homemaking projects such as sewing, cooking, canning, and gardening.

In 1976, the first official Hernando County 4-H agent position was created and filled by Mr. John Weber. In 1980, this position was transitioned to Mr. James Morris and then to Mr. William Hill

in 1983, who served as 4-H agent for fifteen years. In 1999, Ms. Nancy Moores accepted and still maintains the position of Hernando County 4-H agent today. It should be noted that during the interim period between Mr. Hill's transfer to another county position in 1998 and Ms. Moore's induction in 1999, the 4-H program was continued by Ms. Peggy Gist, the only program assistant for Hernando County for the last thirty years.

Though livestock and homemaking projects have continued to thrive and remain prominent projects within the Hernando County 4-H Program, in the 1970s and 1980s, while American and world

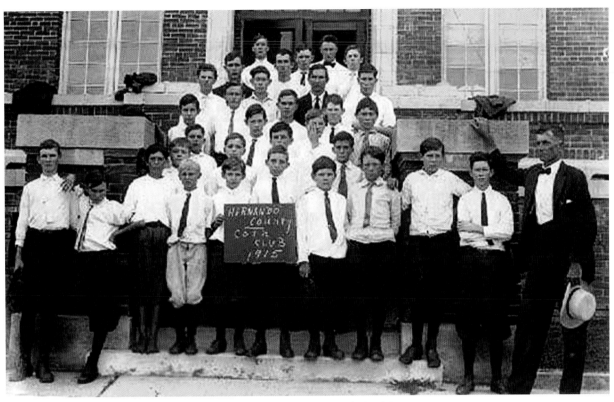

Hernando County 4-H Corn Club, 1915

focuses diversified and expanded, so did the projects and interests within 4-H. New areas of interest arose and generated growth in projects including but not limited to environmental and habitat protection, public speaking, shooting sports, and many competitive projects. Hernando County 4-H members are a competitive group and have been extremely successful within the last decade in earning a place in national competitions, including but not limited to shooting sports, poultry judging, horse, WHEP, and livestock judging. Of special note, Hernando County is also one of only a few counties in Florida that still boasts a sewing construction project.

While club membership numbers have decreased somewhat over the last quarter of a century, Hernando County continues to impress upon the public the need to engage youth in 4-H and the positive learning experiences it offers. Many of the Hernando County leaders have been involved with

4-H for fifteen to thirty years and have maintained a growing base of youth within their clubs year after year. There are four primary clubs that have a long history within the county. Blanche Cambric Academy 4-H Club began in the early 1980s, and has been led by Ms. Helen Fleming for the past fifteen years. The Pony Express 4-H Club began in the '70s as Silver Spurs 4-H Horse and Poultry Club, and has been led by Ms. Dorothy Blair for the last sixteen years. The Hawks 4-H Club was established in the mid-'80s and has been led by Ms. Sillar Townsend for twenty-three years.

The longest-running club under its original name is Future Cattleman 4-H Club, which was established as the Steer Stuffers 4-H Club in the mid-'70s and took on the permanent name of Future Cattleman 4-H Club in 1978. The club was started by Ms. Sarah Waldron as a livestock club focusing on projects for steer and swine. In 1982, the club was transferred into the hands of Ms. Gloria Roller, who

Oliver Fowler feeding his eight-month-old gilt. Hernando County, 1918.

Michael Roller with the buyer of his steer, Mr. Mark Maffett, at the 1983 Youth Steer Show and Sale. (Gloria Roller-Bohannon, photographer)

maintained her organizational leadership role for eighteen years. During that time, she was recognized as Florida's Volunteer of the Year in 1998. In 2000, Gloria handed over the reins to her daughter and Future Cattleman 4-H alumna, Torina Schmidt, who leads the club today; however, Gloria has continued as co-leader for Future Cattleman and celebrated her twenty-fifth year of service to the youth of Hernando County in 2008. Though Future Cattleman 4-H Club still primarily focuses on livestock projects, Schmidt, who has been involved in 4-H since the tender age of six, recognizes that it is important to encourage all youth to become involved with 4-H and therefore does not limit its membership or any area of project interest.

Hernando County 4-H is proud of its long heritage and commitment to serving the community. Community service and helping others is one of the core values that are encouraged within the program. The 4-H clubs have participated every year in various community service events such as cancer walks, collecting suitcases for foster kids, Air Potato, Earth Day and

The Hernando County 4-H leader poses with former Hernando County 4-H Agent Bill Hill after being formally recognized as 1998's Florida 4-H Volunteer of the Year. (Torina Schmidt, photographer)

Hernando County 4-H members Cody Sikes and Amy Roller work on their community service project to beautify the fairgrounds, 1989. (Gloria Roller-Bohannon, photographer)

Beach Day clean-up, adopting needy families for holidays, Toys for Tots drives, recycling cell phones for the Sheriff's Department Domestic Violence Intervention Program, sending holiday cards to the military troops, reading enrichment programs, babysitting for the children of military troops going through orientation, and many more.

HIGHLANDS COUNTY
BY: APRIL BUTLER, TIM HURNER, AND GAYLE JOHNSON

Highlands County has a long, rich history of 4-H, beginning in the 1940s with the first agent, Louis Alsmeyer. News articles dating back to the 1950s describe the construction of Camp Cloverleaf with the Highlands County 4-H agent sitting on the planning committee. The past seven decades document a regular change in 4-H agent leadership and the service of countless dedicated leaders. It is clear that many local leaders can claim their 4-H background in Highlands County as a stepping stone to their present-day success.

CAMPS

Girls had a wonderful time attending the camp to learn about electricity at Camp Ocala. At Camp Cloverleaf, Highlands County 4-H'ers enjoy their week at camp with outdoor activities, skits, and songs.

Highlands County has hosted their own sewing camp as well as livestock judging camps. In 2008, the county is planning a weeklong environmental camp for the youth of the county.

In 2007, the Highlands County 4-H agent, leaders, and the County Council volunteered their time to help at the fiftieth anniversary of Camp Cloverleaf. It seems that camping is timeless in Highlands County.

COUNTY COUNCIL

An article dated in the 1970s describes the 4-H Progress Report given to the county

Dairy exhibit, Highlands County

93

commissioners by 4-H members. Highlands County Council still provides this progress report every year during National 4-H Week; however, they have expanded the event by providing breakfast for the commissioners and other county officials.

Currently, the Highlands County Council is actively involved in District Council, State Congress, and planning county events such as Adopt-A-Grandparent, Highlands County 4-H Olympics, Highlands County Farm City Day, County Awards Night, and officers training for all 4-H officers in the county.

Awards night seems to be a time-tested event with Highlands County 4-H.

In 2007, the theme for Awards Night was *Charlotte's Web*. The County Council wanted to acknowledge what the movie *Charlotte's Web* had done for the 4-H community. Awards were given out for record books, Performance Standard Awards, the "I Dare You" award, and "Friend of 4-H" award.

CLUBS AND PROJECTS

The longest-running club in Highlands County is the Lorida Livestock. The club has been active for thirty-two years. In the early years, Highlands developed project clubs like sewing, cooking, and livestock, but over time, the clubs have evolved into community clubs.

Sewing and clothing construction and selection have found their niche with Highlands County 4-H'ers over the years. Time has not changed the Sewing Program much. Highlands County 4-H holds sewing class every other Monday. The program includes basic to advanced sewing classes open to all youth in the county. They have completed projects such as pillowcases, quilts, and evening gowns. The youth still display the sewing projects at the county fair, and enter into other contests including State Fair and State Congress.

Livestock continues to be a major economic resource for Highlands County. The 4-H program has been involved from early on, from exhibiting animals at the County Fair to hosting the Area E Horse Show at the county horse arena. The 4-H clubs help improve these projects each year by holding livestock camps and clinics and prospect shows, and are currently rejuvenating areas such as livestock judging.

Highlands County Livestock Show

Citrus is one of largest agricultural commodities in Highlands County. The citrus growers and Highlands County Extension have been committed for over ten years to youth citrus projects. The project started with growing a citrus tree and evolved into educational workshops, poster boards, trees, and record books, with the percentage of youth involved in the project increasing every year.

Highlands County 4-H has been established for over sixty-five years and continues to inspire, educate, and establish family morals for youth in Highlands County.

Volunteer Rose Sapp demonstrates the art of sewing to a young 4-H'er, February 2008.

HILLSBOROUGH COUNTY
BY: HOLLY JORDAN, JACQUELINE HUNTER, AND BRENT BROADDUS

The 4-H club in Hillsborough County has been an ever-changing program since its beginning in the early 1900s. Having to meet the needs of both an urban and rural county has been an ongoing challenge that is still faced today. Amid all of the changes that have taken place throughout the decades, and the modification of delivery modes used to reach an ever-changing clientele, the Hillsborough County 4-H Program still maintains the club tradition and mission from the early years.

The roots of the 4-H program in Hillsborough started in 1912 with the founding of tomato and corn clubs, which were coordinated through what is known today as the Extension Service. These programs fell under the direction of Miss Mollie Evers of Plant City. Her annual salary during this

time was $150, which she used to purchase canning supplies and train fare. She later attended training in Tallahassee, Florida, where she was granted the position as the first home demonstration agent. She was fully trained in the preservation of food in tin cans. Her purchase order of 6,000 tin cans was the first for the state Extension Program.

Girls who were members of the tomato clubs would preserve and can the surplus of tomatoes grown in the county. These clubs met at individuals' homes, which were usually near a train station. Boys worked in similar clubs known as corn clubs. These clubs were coordinated by Jack Peters and Tom Kelly, who served in positions that later became known as the county agriculture agents. They focused on production agriculture, mostly swine projects. Many of the 4-H clubs that were

95

Members of the Central Park 4-H Club working on a cooking project, circa 1950.

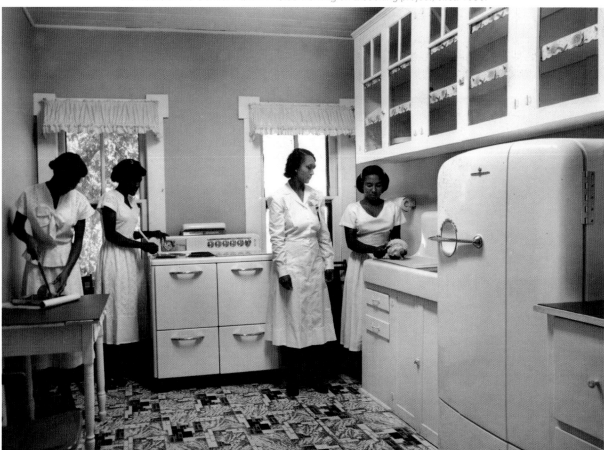

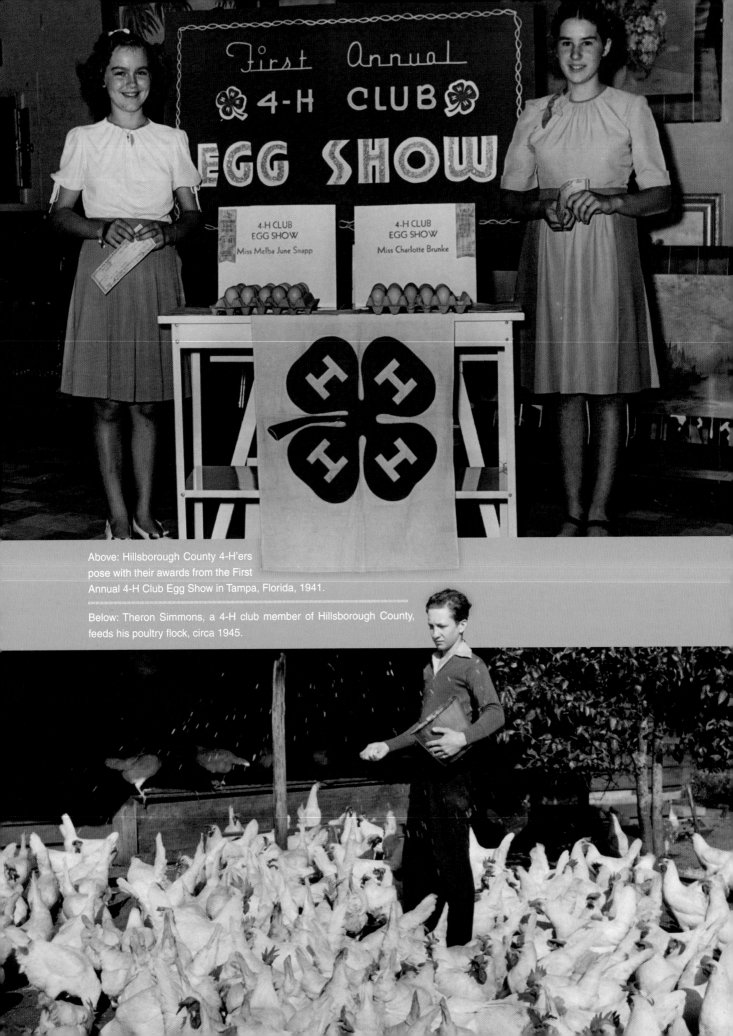

Above: Hillsborough County 4-H'ers pose with their awards from the First Annual 4-H Club Egg Show in Tampa, Florida, 1941.

Below: Theron Simmons, a 4-H club member of Hillsborough County, feeds his poultry flock, circa 1945.

established during this time were started in the schools and the club titles were based on the town in which they met, such as the Brandon 4-H Club or Seffner 4-H Club.

The Hillsborough County 4-H Program celebrated its twenty-fifth anniversary in 1939. At that time, there were two Extension Offices located in the county (established in 1919): one in Tampa and the other in Plant City. A third office in Ruskin, Florida, was established in 1951. Agriculture and home demonstration agents were housed at each of these offices, where they focused on conducting programs in their designated location based on the immediate needs of the residents of those areas. For example, the eastern Hillsborough 4-H clubs were organized and met in the schools in Plant City, Florida. The rural schools of that area, commonly known as "Strawberry Schools," scheduled their school terms and 4-H programs to conform to the strawberry harvest season of January through March. This was necessary because most family members in the Plant City area were needed to help out with harvesting the strawberry crops during peak production months.

Typical 4-H events during the 1930s included showing livestock at the fairs and participating in land, livestock, and citrus judging contests. The 4-H events for girls included sewing and cooking projects and contests such as dishwashing, sandwich-making, posture, and table-setting.

During the late 1930s and early 1940s, 4-H programs adapted to the changing needs of families due to the impact of the war. In Hillsborough, projects that were traditionally reserved for the boys, such as livestock, gardening, and dairy, were now being required as part of the county club programs for the girls. In the early 1940s, the requirements for girls enrolled in the 4-H program included

studying clothing as well as one production project (beekeeping, gardening, poultry, dairy, or livestock). More changes came during the onset of the war, as many of the boys who were graduating from high school were soon sent overseas for the war effort. Many did not have the opportunity at that time to enroll in college.

The focus of the Hillsborough Extension Service agriculture and home demonstration agents also shifted away from 4-H and more toward priority special war programs during this time, which were eventually terminated in 1945. Even with the shift toward the war effort, the 4-H program still managed to implement new programs during this time, such as the first 4-H Achievement Day, the first 4-H club Dairy Show coordinated by the Tampa Chamber of Commerce (January 10, 1947), and the first Junior Agriculture Show for 4-H boys, girls, and FFA members (December 18, 1946). In addition, Miss Floy Britt, home demonstration agent from Florida A&M University, came to Hillsborough County in 1940 to work with African-American clients in Plant City, Citrus Park, Sulfur Springs, Port Tampa, Bealsville, and Seffner.

The 1950s and 1960s were a time of great social change for 4-H members. Boys' and girls' 4-H club programs, which were kept separate in prior years, were now starting to be coordinated together. Although the boys and girls still met in separate 4-H clubs, they hosted and planned social events together such as picnics, parties, and wiener roasts. In 1965, boys and girls from Hillsborough County participated in overnight camping trips together. Another major trend during this decade was the increasing number and availability of 4-H programs focused on urban youth who did not have an agricultural background. This also included programs for African-American youth in the early 1960s. Sudella Ford, home economics

97

Toni Vernon and Cooky Gaines participate at the State 4-H Dairy Show, Orlando, Florida, 1960.

agent, worked with the African-American 4-H clubs in Hillsborough County. The two largest African-American clubs at that time in the county were located in Bealsville and Citrus Park. Although these clubs were segregated from the white clubs in the county, 4-H members came together at the Florida State Fair, where African-American and white girls participated in the fashion show together.

In addition to the social changes that were taking place during this time, there was a shift in the responsibility of the 4-H program. The program that was previously coordinated by both agriculture and home demonstration agents together was brought under the leadership of what is known today as the county 4-H agent. Virginia Hill Coombs was the first agent in Hillsborough County whose full responsibility was management of the 4-H program. To complete this era of the program, the first 4-H Tropicana Public Speaking Contest was held in 1969 for Hillsborough County, which continues today. The 4-H Expanded Food and Nutrition Education Program was added as well, and continues to teach nutrition to youth

in limited-resource areas throughout Hillsborough County.

In 1974, the three offices of the Extension Service all merged together at a central headquarters in Seffner, Florida. This office still houses the Hillsborough County Extension Service today. This changed the 4-H program in that the agents were no longer housed in the "backyard" of the clients with which they worked, although they still had the same mission as in earlier years. Also during the 1970s, more clubs shifted out of the schools and into the local community, which is our current method of club delivery today.

Later, into the 1980s and 1990s, many new and innovative 4-H programs were established to reach clientele who were not part of the traditional club program. Programs such as the Ag-Venture Program, school enrichment, Seat Belt Safety contest, grant programs (recycling and water conservation), and Weed and Seed reach non-traditional 4-H members in urban and rural areas.

Many of these programs are still in place today with the addition of the Operation Military Kids Program and 4-H clubs at MacDill Airforce Base. Clubs still maintain their original roots and continue to meet throughout the county, but the greatest concentration is still in eastern and southern Hillsborough County, where 4-H club projects tend to be agriculturally based. Even with the many social and organizational changes, the 4-H program in Hillsborough County continues its mission to teach youth through "learn by doing" methods with the goal to "make the best better."

HOLMES COUNTY
BY: NICOLE CRAWSON

Holmes County was established in 1848 with a population of approximately 1,205. The earliest reports of 4-H in the county, as published in the local paper *Holmes County Times*, date back to January 10, 1930, when "Edna Burgess won first prize for North Florida" and received $25 given by the Chilean Nitrate of Soda Educational Bureau for her gardening efforts. Under the leadership of Home Demonstration Agent Bettie Caudle, Holmes County 4-H flourished for many years. As mentioned in the article "Holmes Wins Club Honors," published by the *Holmes County Times* on January 17, 1930, "Mrs. Caudle has summed up the situation and is able to say that it has been the best year ever. Due to all [4-H] events, the women and girls give Holmes the grand championship and sweepstakes record for the State of Florida."

Undoubtedly, Holmes County 4-H was considered one of the most successful leaders of its time in the 4-H club world. As written by a local citizen, Spuds Johnson, in the "Rural Common Sense" article in the *Holmes County Times* on Friday, November 25, 1932, "First of all, last year when everything was having hard growing, boys' 4-H club enrollment increased about 20%. They are now nearly 2,500 strong in Florida." Johnson further stated, "Club work is being carried on in 33 counties in Florida and I am proud that the farm boys in our county have the advantage of it."

Further research found in 1940 that Holmes County 4-H continued to grow strong. A local ad called for a 4-H council meeting at the courthouse: "Members from 21 clubs of the county are expected to assemble for the business session when plans will be discussed for the new year." Later that same year, an article stated that Mrs. Bettie Caudle's "Bethlehem 4-H girls reported 30 fruit trees and 18 rose bushes had been planted since their last meeting."

Current 4-H Agent Nicole Crawson had a pleasant conversation with a long-time resident of Holmes County, Ms. Sybil Taylor, age eighty-three. Taylor, with a sharp and witty mind, recalled numerous

A young Holmes County 4-H'er with livestock, February 1963

4-H events and activities that she participated in as a Holmes County youth. She remembers Mrs. Bettie Caudle being her 4-H leader as the home demonstration agent and that she was good at putting you on the spot to keep you in line. "Mrs. Bettie was efficient and thorough but if she saw you doing anything that wasn't up to standards, she wouldn't say a word to you. But, just let the next club meeting day come along, and she'd say, 'I want you to know that I was at this lady's home and she did so and so.'"

The discussion soon drifted back to 1932, when Taylor took out her own handmade 4-H apron with the famous clover clearly embroidered on it, all in pristine condition. According to Taylor, the apron was the first thing she ever made in 4-H, at eight or nine years old. It took her no more than five minutes to make it, as she rushed to complete the project. Made out of a flour sack, as that was all her mother could gather at the time, the material already had a hole in it so she had to patch it before she could sew the apron. However, because she rushed through the project, Caudle informed her that she needed to take the apron apart and start over since the stitching was too big. According to Taylor, she had to re-stitch her apron several times to get Caudle's approval. Taylor said she must have made that apron nine times before she got it just right! "I about got it worn out before I got it made."

In addition to her lovely 4-H apron, Taylor shared a story about attending 4-H Camp Timpoochee, one of the first 4-H residential camps in the nation, established in 1926. Referring back to 1936, when she was just twelve, Taylor recalled her camp experience and humorously referred to the memory with a small giggle as the highlight of her childhood, but "it had a lemon in it." With smiling eyes and a sharp, vivid memory, Taylor recalled wanting to go to 4-H camp and needing to bring a dressed chicken as the registration fee that year in order to go. She said dressing a chicken was no problem for her, as she lived on a farm and her daddy had taught her how to do that years before. Unfortunately, right before she was to go to camp, a family member that lived in south Florida died and her mother had to go to the funeral. Taylor said she wasn't planning on going to camp after that but, at the very last minute on the day the camp bus was going by, her older sister talked her into going after all. She and her sister didn't think they had time to dress the chicken before the bus came, so her sister told her to bring a live chicken

to camp, tell Mrs. Bettie Caudle about it, and she'd let her dress it there. So, with the decision made on the spot by her older sister, Taylor says she eased onto the camp bus with her live chicken in her crocker sack.

Ms. Sybil Taylor, age eighty-three, displaying her homemade 4-H apron from 1932.

As the bus took off for Camp Timpoochee, unexpectedly, and unfortunately for a shy, young girl at the time, some of the boys on the bus got rowdy and kicked her crocker sack. Taylor says her chicken began squawking loudly and the boys were entertained for the remainder of the trip by teasing her about bringing a live chicken to camp. As Taylor so eloquently put it, "I was a sensitive child anyway, and that liked to have killed me. If they had stopped that bus, I would have gotten off and walked back home gladly." When they finally arrived at camp, she was devastated. When the

Holmes County 4-H and FFA fair
exhibits, 1960s

Holmes County senior 4-H members, February 1963

further stated, "I thought, well, if these children are doing me this way, and the way Ms. Bettie Caudle can take you apart, I'm not facing her with it!" Fortunately, Taylor got to stay the week at camp and no one said another word about her live chicken until her last night at camp, when Caudle began the night with, "I want you to know that some camper here brought her live chicken and left it on the bus and I had to clean it!" As Taylor said, "Ms. Bettie would make a point of letting you know that she knew what you did, without having to say your name!"

Today, Holmes County 4-H still participates in the tradition of Camp Timpoochee. Currently, Holmes County 4-H is in a restructuring and regrowth phase under the direction of 4-H Agent Nicole Crawson. Although Holmes County 4-H is seeing smaller numbers than those from the past, the successful development of positive life skills in youth is still a major part of the rural program.

bus came to a stop, she jumped off that bus and left her chicken behind. One of the boys came up to her and tried to give her the chicken back. She said she left that chicken with him because she "didn't want anything more to do with it." She

INDIAN RIVER COUNTY

In 2007, Indian River 4-H enrolled 3,317 youth in 4,101 projects. Indian River County is host to twenty-six 4-H clubs and 263 adult volunteers. After-school programming is strong in Indian River County 4-H, where the Ag in the Classroom project is the most popular. Other major projects in 2007 were wildlife and fisheries and public speaking.

State 4-H Council officers, 2005–2006. From left to right are: Vice President Tyler Carstensen, Osceola County; President Abigail Crawford, Bradford County; Parliamentarian Sandy Bass, Indian River County; Secretary Jean Leifhelm, Indian River County; reporter April Lacasse, Flagler County; historian Danielle Padgett, Sarasota County; and sergeant-at-arms Jackson Mullins, Santa Rosa County. (Not pictured: Treasurer Mylo Cheng, Palm Beach County.)

JACKSON COUNTY
BY: PATTI PEACOCK

Ask any long-time resident of Jackson County what they remember about 4-H, and most will smile and say, "4-H Camp Timpoochee!" Newspaper archives show 4-H activities beginning in the mid-1920s, but the program really took off in the '30s. One 4-H alum, Mrs. Billy (Wester) Dickson of Grand Ridge, says her earliest memories of 4-H began in the 1940s and had strong ties to her mother's homemaker club, The Willing Workers. Because the mothers brought their children with them to monthly meetings, they decided to sponsor a 4-H club. Mrs. Bonnie J. Carter was the first club leader, and taught everything from sewing to canning. Dickson recalls her most memorable 4-H moment, when she won first place at state for her food and nutrition demonstration in 1948. It made her proud to board a steam locomotive headed for Chicago, Illinois, to compete at the National 4-H Congress. Dickson shared, "although I did not win, it will always be a treasured memory."

Earliest records show that Ms. Aleyne Heath served as the 4-H/home economics agent from 1930 to 1950. After Heath, Mary Bennet and Jane Burgess worked with 4-H youth. During the time of segregation, the county hired Mr. Virgil Elkins to work with minority youth. Once he was promoted to the state office, Mrs. Pearl Long was hired as the minority agent for home economics and 4-H in 1960. During her service to Extension, she recalled traveling to every minority school and teaching programs on public speaking and teen nutrition. The youth were so receptive, that often they had to meet in gyms or auditoriums. One of her favorite memories was of taking youth to compete at the state fair. One year, she had to charter two buses instead of one! Once there, 4-H'ers

competed in demonstrations, public speaking, and judging contests.

Camp Timpoochee

During the period of segregation, minority youth traveled to Camp Dove, not far from 4-H Camp Ocala. In the 1960s, youth worked on many of the same projects that we have today. One of the most popular projects was building a reading lamp from a cypress knee. Once integration began, Long was offered a job with Extension in DeLand, but declined because she did not want to relocate her family. She shared that, "Extension was the best job I ever had… I loved all the information from the specialists, and I felt that I learned just as much as the kids did."

Over the past seventy years, Jackson County 4-H'ers have made many accomplishments; unfortunately, not all of them have been recorded, but from personal interviews and recollections, we have pieced together major accomplishments from each decade:

103

Mary Lou Weeler with a suit made for the clothing demonstration

Jackson County first-place Livestock Judging team. Florida State Fair, 1960.

- 1940s – Aleyne Heath served as the home economics and 4-H Extension agent. Billy Wester (first place in state food and nutrition demonstration) and Emma Neil Lawrence (first place in state clothing demonstration) competed in the National 4-H Congress in Chicago, Illinois.

- 1950s – Mary Bennet and Jane Burgess served as the home economics and 4-H agents working with white youth. Virgil Elkins worked with minority 4-H'ers, and produced numerous state-winning judging teams. Mrs. John Alter was crowned the State Dairy Queen.

- 1960s – Jane Burgess continued to serve as the 4-H agent, and Mrs. Pearl Long was hired to work with minority youth. During this time, Jackson County 4-H'ers won several public speaking, demonstration, and judging contests at the State and North Florida Fairs; Wendell Taylor was the first-place high individual at the State Livestock Judging Contest, and also served as a lifeguard at 4-H Camp Timpoochee.

- 1970s – Jackson County's first full-time 4-H agent, Marvin Barnes, was hired. Janice McElroy won first place in public speaking at 4-H State Congress.

- 1980s – Sheila (Munsey) Andreason was hired as the next 4-H agent. With her help, two of our longest-running clubs were formed: the Horsing Around 4-H Club and the Lovedale 4-H Club.

- 1990s – Mrs. Andreason led several teams of youth to win state and national judging contests in poultry, livestock judging, forestry, and wildlife. Heather (Schultz) Kent was hired as the new 4-H agent in 1999.

- 2000–present – In 2002, Colonel Wendell Taylor was inducted into the Florida 4-H Hall of Fame. Bryce Melvin served as the 4-H District II president and attended National 4-H Congress in 2004. In 2006, Brittany Peacock won first place in the State 4-H Fashion Revue. In 2008, Mrs. Patty Melvin, leader of the 4-H Character Keepers Club, was awarded the Florida 4-H Lifetime Volunteer Award.

JEFFERSON COUNTY
BY: JOHN LILLY AND HINES BOYD

At the beginning of the twentieth century, Jefferson County was one of Florida's larger counties and had a thriving agricultural economy. It was a natural incubator for the 4-H club programs, which the new agricultural Extension Service began to promote in the early 1900s.

In Jefferson County, and throughout the nation, the goal of the early agricultural Extension pioneers was to disseminate new agricultural production technology gleaned from the research efforts of the land grant colleges. Farmers often resisted these new ideas. Extension leaders felt that one way to reach resistant farmers (and their wives) was through the children of farm families. So they began organizing "project clubs" through which they could educate and train young people. Not only might the new ideas spill over to their parents, but many of these young people would also become the farmers and homemakers of tomorrow.

Unfortunately, most of the archives and records of Jefferson County's 4-H early programs and activities have been lost. To reconstruct parts of the history, we have depended heavily on the recollections of an agricultural family that first settled in Jefferson County in the 1830s. The Finlayson-Boyd family still farms in Jefferson County today and has been close to 4-H since its early days. Below are some snapshots of Jefferson County 4-H history as seen through the eyes of three generations of this family.

John Finlayson was a young boy in the early 1930s Depression era when his father, Ed Finlayson, served as County Extension agent. Though John was too young to have his own "project," he remembers the involvement of his older brother, Ed, in a corn club and pig club. Pigs were popular because most farm families did not feel they could devote a beef animal to a "kid's project" during the hard times of the Depression.

While 4-H club activities were usually segregated by sex and race during this period, John recalls some distinct exceptions. John's brother, Ed, partnered with a young African-American neighbor friend, "Shot" Gee, in a corn project. When they were dividing the money from the sale of their corn, Ed and Shot had a nickel left over with no way to divide it, so they gave it to John for his help. Shot's project was supervised by Miles Groover, the Extension agent for African-American farm families. John recalls him as a "very smart man."

Though pigs and corn were usually the domain of the boys, a neighboring girl soon insisted on joining the pig club so that she could "sell" her project, too. Her pig club membership was an exception. The girls of that period usually worked sewing, canning, and gardening projects.

Miss Ruby Brown, Jefferson County's home demonstration agent during the 1930s, worked especially hard on gardening and canning projects for "her girls." The products that they canned became the food supply for the summer 4-H Camping Program during those tough days of the Depression.

Since the 1920s, camping programs have been an important part of 4-H life. Camp Timpoochee on Choctahatchee Bay near current-day Destin was Florida's first 4-H camp and one of the first in the

105

nation. Jefferson County camped there before Camp Cherry Lake was opened in the late 1930s.

Finlayson recalls a harrowing experience for Jefferson County 4-H'ers while they were at Camp Timpoochee during the summer of 1936. On August 1, a hurricane with ninety- to one-hundred-mile-per-hour winds took aim directly at the camp. The camp staff included Billy Mathews and Wilmer Bassett. (Mathews was later a long-time U.S. Congressman. Bassett moved on to be a well-known Jefferson County dairyman and major 4-H benefactor. Both men are members of the Florida 4-H Hall of Fame.)

Extension Agent Albert Odom with a group of 4-H boys on their way to a 4-H event.

Because there wasn't enough warning to evacuate the camp, Mathews and Bassett loaded the campers and leaders onto the school buses that had brought them there. They parked the buses in the large field in the center of the camp, away from trees and facing the wind. As the eye of the storm move through, they reoriented the buses. The plan worked for everyone—except the camp cook, who refused to get on the bus. After the storm passed, the staff found the cook in the camp kitchen in his oven. Though a few cabins were blown off their foundations, everyone was safe, including the cook.

By the 1950s, 4-H had evolved from "project clubs" to mostly school-based clubs. Albert Odom, the county agent, aggressively organized these school clubs. The "projects" not only included crops and livestock, but subjects like electricity and farm safety. Albert Odom emphasized social and leadership development skills, which included public speaking, judging teams,

and leadership councils. He spent long hours exposing his "farm boys" to training and trips that expanded their horizons, recalls Hines Boyd, one of the beneficiaries of Odom's tireless efforts and constant affirmation.

Since Odom was the only agricultural agent in the county (though Mary McCloud and, later, Fern Nix acted as home demonstration agents), there was grumbling about the amount of time he spent with 4-H programs. The complaints led one county commissioner to take aim at his job. But Albert Odom had many young allies. Boyd remembers going to see several commissioners to be sure they understood the benefits of Odom's work. The campaign was a success. Albert Odom kept his job and his influence on the youth he served, one of whom was U.S. Congressman Allen Boyd.

The integration of the public schools in the late 1960s and the urbanization of Florida dramatically changed the face of 4-H. Clubs were moved from the schools to community clubs dependent on

Hines Boyd, third from left, receives a 4-H check sponsored by Winn-Dixie, 1960.

Jefferson 4-H County Council, roadside clean-up, 2007

Soon, with the encouragement of Lilly and some 4-H camping friends, Beth attended 4-H Legislature, a hands-on Youth Civics Training Program that began in the 1970s. Beth became increasingly involved in leadership programs, winning the state 4-H public speaking contest and later a position as a State 4-H Council officer. During her 4-H years, she never missed a summer at Camp Cherry Lake. By the age of sixteen, she was a camp staff intern and was soon offered a summer-long position on the camp staff, her first paid job. She ended her 4-H career at age twenty as the camp program coordinator, where she supervised five workers—her first supervisory experience.

Looking back ten years later, Beth Boyd Nunnally, now the mother of two girls and a regional director of a large health care company, credits much of her success to her 4-H experience and the encouragement of 4-H leaders like John Lilly.

volunteer adult leaders. Programs were modified to also benefit youth who were not from agricultural families.

Beth, Hines Boyd's daughter, recalls beginning her 4-H career at age nine when she enrolled in a summer sewing class taught by home demonstration agent Phyllis Kennedy. She liked the class so well that she participated in a microwave cooking and bread-making class the next summer. It was 1988, and long-time 4-H Agent John Lilly had just arrived in Jefferson County.

Beth's experience illustrates the transformation that 4-H has made in the last four decades, from an organization focused mostly on agricultural projects to a rural/urban youth development organization. Today, Jefferson County still has its Ag-Adventure Club with an emphasis on agricultural projects and judging teams. In other clubs, young people learn useful life skills like cooking, sewing, gardening, and landscaping, skills that are no longer taught in schools. And there are plenty of opportunities for developing social and leadership skills.

LAFAYETTE COUNTY
BY: JANA HART

The Lafayette County 4-H Program has been active, growing, and changing throughout the past century. Over the years, the program has continued the traditional values as well as adapted to the changing world that we are in. Lafayette 4-H'ers have always participated in livestock programs, showing hogs, steers, and poultry at area fairs, as well as camping at 4-H Camp Cherry Lake over the summer. Community clubs have been active for decades in a variety of projects, mostly giving children leadership opportunities in small groups.

In the past twenty-five years, Lafayette County commissioners, seeing a growing 4-H program, added a classroom at the Agricultural Complex specifically for the 4-H Summer Environmental Program. The six-week day camps are held during the summer and focus on environmental education. Lafayette 4-H was also responsible for the original Recycling Awareness programs that started in the county in the 1980s. The 4-H'ers distributed recycling bins and educational materials to all Mayo residents, encouraging them to participate

Florida Boys' 4-H Council officers. Tampa, Florida, February 18, 1961. From left to right, front row: Dr. M. O. Watkins, director of Extension; Glen Mixson, Lake Placid; Stoney Stoutamire, Bristol; Jacky Strickland, Gainesville; Hines Boyd, Greenville; Willard M. Fifield, provost for agriculture; and K. D. Ripper, Maas Brothers, Tampa. Back row: D. Colin Lindsey, Belk-Lindsey, Tampa; Wayne Ezell, Mayo; Skippy Lambert, Cantonment; Bert Ashton, West Palm Beach; Sam Baker, New Port Richey; Bill Nelson, Melbourne; and James E. Gorman, Florida Retail Federation, Jacksonville.

in the countywide Recycling Program. In 2000, Lafayette 4-H received a seed grant to start an After-school Program at the Lafayette Elementary School for children who would have been home alone and needed additional care after school. That program was a huge success and is still going strong years after the grant ended.

Currently, Lafayette 4-H'ers enjoy participating in county, district, and state events, including demonstrations, Share-the-Fun, and public speaking. In the last quarter-century, many Lafayette 4-H'ers have broadened their horizons by participating in National 4-H Congress, Citizenship Washington Focus, Citizenship World Focus, American Heritage, and Florida's 4-H Legislature. From these and other traditional 4-H experiences, Lafayette 4-H alumni have improved the quality of their life, their families, and their community. As we look back and remember the past hundred years, we have confidence as we look forward to a bright future for Lafayette 4-H.

LAKE COUNTY
BY: CORDELLA LaROE

In Lake County, the first boys' clubs came to Florida in 1910, while girls' clubs began in the state in 1912. The earliest-known photographic existence of the 4-H program dates back to 1913, when a girls' delegation represented Lake County at a short course in Tallahassee. During these early years, Lake County 4-H boys were led by the county agricultural agent and the girls by the home demonstration agent. Throughout the years, the variety of projects grew, but clubs were still segregated by race and gender.

The first county agricultural agent was Jack Peters. He was appointed in 1912 and served for twenty months. He was followed by William Gomme (1914–1918) and M. M. Javens (1918–1920). The first home demonstration agent was Cora Peat, who was appointed in 1915 and served for one year. She was followed by Clarine Hoyt (1917–1919), Ora Odom (1922–1923), and Marie Cox-King (1923–1927).

As one of the first agents, Miss Cox-King organized twenty-one girls' 4-H clubs. At that time, girls' clubs focused on clothing, poultry, and food and nutrition, while the boys' projects centered on livestock, tractor maintenance, beekeeping, and citrus production. In 1964, 4-H was officially racially integrated, and in 1969, girls and boys could be members of the same club.

Lake County boys at Camp McQuarrie, 1950s

Lake County 4-H has a long-standing tradition of members attending short courses: girls in Tallahassee, boys in Gainesville. Photographs reveal numerous delegations over many years. This tradition continues today with large numbers of Lake County members attending events throughout the state and nation.

Lake County 4-H Club girls' trip to the short course in Tallahassee, 1937

Altoona 4-H Club boys make cuttings for a school beautification project, December 12, 1951.

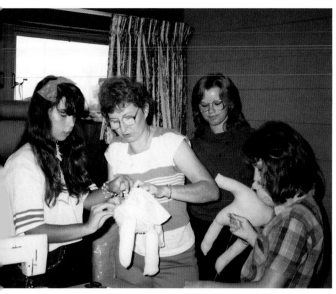
Cordella LaRoe teaches sewing.

Golden Triangle (1970–2008), and Conant Farmers (1982–2008). These clubs have changed leaders and locations over the years but the name, purpose, and location have always stayed the same.

Lake County 4-H has been honored with inductions into the Florida 4-H Hall of Fame. Barbara Eveland and Louise Cox were both inducted in 2002. Miss Cox and Mrs. Eveland were long-time leaders and each kept 4-H close to her heart. Most recently, Cordella and Gene LaRoe were inducted to the 4-H Hall of Fame (2007) for their continued support and involvement in the Lake County 4-H Program.

Throughout time, Lake County has evolved and changed, focusing on community needs and interests. Membership in the program has continued to increase and involvement in county, district, state, and national attendance has remained strong. As the one hundredth anniversary of the Lake County 4-H Program draws near, we hope to continue making the best better and develop the program as a respectable and solid youth development organization.

The program has evolved over the years and now includes a high enrollment in livestock, horses, citizenship and leadership, and shooting sports projects. The 4-H club offers more than one hundred different projects and involves a diverse group of youth from rural, suburban, and urban lifestyles. While clubs have come and gone, three clubs have graduated 4-H members for over twenty years: Montverde 4-H (1945–2005),

111

LEE COUNTY
BY: BOBBI HARRISON

Lee County, located on the banks of the Caloosahatchee River in Southwest Florida, has a rich 4-H history. The first 4-H club was formed in the 1920s on Pine Island as a cattle club and was started by the agriculture agent. The club became non-functional during the Depression due to the closure of the Extension Office during this difficult economic time, but after the Depression, 4-H came back with renewed strength.

During the 1960s and 1970s, the program took off with youth participating in livestock, horse, small

animals, home economics, and public speaking projects. Many youth showcased their projects at the South West Florida Fair. The fairgrounds were located at Terry Park until 1977, when it was relocated to the Lee Civic Center. Terry Park then became the permanent site of the Lee County Extension Service, where the office is currently located.

Lee County hired the first 4-H agent in 1972, while the longest-running 4-H club is Lee Livestock, which has been a functioning club for over thirty

Southwest Florida Fair. Robin Stanley of the 4-H Beef Cattle Club exhibits "Big Boy," who sold for $1.80 per pound, 1971.

years. Many current youth in the club are third-generation Lee County 4-H members. Terri Thomas, Denise Parker, and Teresa Mann are the current leaders of the club.

Lee's most distinguished 4-H alumni is Douglas Molloy, who holds the distinguished title of chief assistant United States attorney for the U.S. Attorney's Office Middle District of Florida. As a 4-H youth, he participated in public speaking competitions, 4-H Legislature, and the 4-H youth County Council, District Council, and State Executive Boards. He attributes his success today to many of the life skills he learned in 4-H.

Pictured at the top from left to right are Eddie Currie and Robin Stanley; at the bottom from left to right are Teddy White and Mitch Skinner. State Congress, 1972.

The Lee County 4-H Program has grown over the years. Today there are twenty-nine clubs, 450 4-H members, and seventy-five adult volunteers who partner with youth to learn life skills, citizenship, and leadership skills. Lee County also has several traditional 4-H animal science clubs that focus on market animals, horse, small animal, beef breeding, swine, and goat projects. Over 200 4-H youth each year showcase their projects at the South West Florida Fair as they learn entrepreneurial skills.

In addition, youth are actively involved in citizenship and leadership learning activities. They serve as officers in their clubs and on County Council, District Council, and State Executive Boards. They serve as teen camp counselors at Camp Cloverleaf each summer and as teen leaders at the Discover Lee Day Camp. Several youth each year attend State Legislature and Citizenship Washington Focus to learn more about their government. The youth compete at Congress and are encouraged to become lifelong learners. Attending college and turning their project area into a career is strongly encouraged.

Lee County is especially proud of one of its youth, Allison Campbell, who in 2004 was elected

Lee County proclaims National 4-H Week, October 9, 2007. Back row, from left to right, are: Extension Director Celia Hill, Matthew Cooper, Jessica Campbell, Kim Muchmore, Holly Kobie, Jennifer Sites, and Rhonda Tice. Front row: Brenda Cooner, Olivia Muchmore, Victoria Muchmore, Jessica Kobie, and 4-H Agent Cathy Suggs.

to be the State 4-H president presiding over the 4-H youth in Florida at Executives Boards, Legislature, and Congress. Today, she is attending Baylor University and hopes to pursue a career in government.

The Lee County 4-H Program has come a long way from the first cattle club in the 1920s. While the county boasts several strong traditional market animal and horse clubs, they also have teen leadership, marine biology, nutrition, clothing construction, horticulture, and shooting sports clubs. Youth are learning life skills, citizenship, and leadership skills from caring adult volunteers and teen leaders. The program continues to thrive and

one measure of this success is the returning alumni who want their children and grandchildren to join 4-H. Not only do their children and grandchildren join the program, but the alumni also come back to Lee County 4-H as volunteer leaders. The Lee County 4-H Program has influenced many youth over the years to return and give back to their community. They are the hands of 4-H.

LEON COUNTY
BY: TRACY TESDALL

The 4-H Youth Development Program has a long history in the Sunshine State and in Leon County. Exploring 4-H history provides learners with some unique insights on the history of the 4-H movement and the history of our county, our state, and our nation.

The Leon County 4-H Judging Team won the state contest. Pictured from left to right are: Assistant Agent Edsel Thomaston, Pleas Strickland, Virginia Ruff, Don Herold, C. C. Sellers, and Steve Willis of the *Florida Times Union*, who presented the trophy to the youth in Orlando, 1955.

Girls' tomato clubs were started in eleven counties during 1912, including Leon, by Agnes Ellen Harris, the first county home demonstration agent of Leon County, Florida. Miss Harris left her position

as head of home economics at Florida State College for Women in order to become Florida's first home demonstration agent. Each girl planted and harvested tomatoes on a one-tenth-acre plot. The tomato clubs were organized through public schools and the home garden and kitchen served as the laboratory. Home demonstration agents visited rural schools to talk about the tomato clubs, then left enrollment forms with the teachers. After getting their parents' permission to join, the girls completed enrollment cards and mailed them to the home demonstration agent. The agent then sent tomato seed, planting instructions, and a record book to each enrolled member. Until 1914, the home demonstration agent only worked part of the year.

In the fall of 1916, the first group of African-American home demonstration agents were taught canning in tins at the Agricultural and Mechanical College in Tallahassee. The work was conducted mainly through clubs called farm-makers' clubs and homemakers' clubs, in which boys and girls, respectively, participated. The boys cultivated half an acre of corn, one-fourth acre of peanuts, and one-fourth acre of sweet potatoes. The girls grew one-tenth acre of tomatoes and preserved many products from the farm.

In 1923, there were 115 girls and fifteen boys in the Leon County 4-H Program. By the time Mrs. Ruth Kellum resigned in 1933 with ten years of service, she had increased program membership to 190 girls.

County. From November 1923 to April 1933, Ruth Bogardus Conibear Kellum served as the home demonstration agent.

After 1933, the home demonstrations agents included Miss Ethyl Holloway, Mrs. William Roberts, Mrs. Lura Dyer Noland, Mrs. Eva Richardson Culley, and Mrs. Mamie Scott Russell. The boys'

Girls enjoying a cool drink from the canteen. Camp Cherry Lake, 1941.

In 1963, all three 4-H programs (white boys, white girls, and African-American youth) were combined into one program open to all youth in Leon County.

Throughout the years, project work in Leon County included gardening (tomatoes, peanuts, cotton, etc.) crocheting, canning, and livestock projects. Camping at Lake Bradford and annual trips to 4-H camps Cherry Lake and Timpoochee occurred with the white boys and girls. Prior to 1963, African-American boys and girls camped at Doe Lake in the Ocala National Forest. Poultry and embryology seemed to be predominant with the boys' and girls' programs.

Agnes Ellen Harris served as Leon County home demonstration agent beginning in 1912. Home demonstration agents in the early years were responsible for all the 4-H work in Leon

Leon County 4-H environmental education project work dominates the efforts of 4-H members in today's program.

program was led by various agricultural Extension agents, including J. T. Hurst, Frank Robinson, J. A. McIntosh, and G. C. Hodge. Richard Hartsfield was responsible for the African-American boys' and girls' programs for many years beginning in the 1950s. Through the effort of the home demonstration and agriculture agents, the 4-H program flourished in Leon County.

Personnel records are unclear on exactly who did 4-H work during some years; however, it is clear that Mrs. Mamie Daughtry was the home demonstration agent in the 1950s through the '60s. In this time period, the full-time 4-H agent title was established in Leon County. From 1969 to 1972, Ann Paramore was the 4-H agent before becoming a home economics agent. Jane Brody was hired as 4-H agent in 1972; she was followed by Lorraine Sanders in August 1973 through August 1975. In the early '70s, a second full-time 4-H agent, Lawrence Heitmeyer, was brought on to the staff. Elaine C. Shook joined him in September 1975. In 1979, the Leon County Extension 4-H Department was established with Heitmeyer as the 4-H program leader. In 1981, Heitmeyer was promoted to Leon County Extension director and Shook became the 4-H program leader. Between 1981 and 1993, various additional agents were hired in 4-H, including David Dinkins. In November 1993, Marcus D. Boston, Jr. was hired and is on staff today. In December 2005, Shook retired. Tracy A. Tesdall joined Boston in January 2006.

Primary programming in Leon County 4-H ranges from 4-H club development, environmental education, teen leadership programs, talent shows, area horse shows, summer camps (at Camp Cherry Lake), Florida 4-H Legislature, poster and photo contests, forestry and wildlife contests, embryology, babysitting workshops, the North Florida Fair, and the 4-H/Tropicana Public Speaking Program. In 2008, there were twenty-four 4-H clubs with more than 400 club members. An additional 8,000 school-age youth were reached though camping, school enrichment, and special interest programming.

LEVY COUNTY

Levy County 4-H enrolled 1,756 youth in 2,014 projects in the year 2007. The rural Levy County was host to sixty 4-H clubs and had ninety-nine adult volunteers as of 2007. Major projects for Levy County youth are public speaking, shooting sports, and outdoor recreation and education.

The United Nations flag is presented to Bronson School, October 24, 1950. The flag was presented to Principal M. F. Kiester (left) by Shirley Fender (second from right), president of the group. Mrs. Sue Murphy, HAD (behind flag), and Mrs. Walter Duden, president of the Levy County HD Council which sponsored the project, look on.

LIBERTY COUNTY
BY: MORGAN BARNETT

Liberty County is saturated with 4-H history, and has leapt from modest beginnings in the early 1900s to the growing number of youth and agents involved today.

Swine project, 1961

In 1855, Liberty County was created, and in 1917, the 4-H program was formed by Alexander W. Turner. Mr. Turner helped start the first 4-H corn and hog clubs, and was known to work long hours holding short courses and helping both youth and adults learn more about life. He would take the boys to the University of Florida for their 4-H short course one year, and the next year travel with the girls to Florida State College for Women (now known as Florida State University) for their course.

Enrollment numbers in the county's program have had a drastic change. What started as fourteen boys in corn clubs transformed into 107 youth

The 4-H Pepper Contest participants, North Florida Fair. From left to right, back row: Cayla Eikelond, LaBarren Smith, Tyler Stoutamire, and Pauline Boykin. Front row: Marcus Andrews, Vantessa McCraye, and Jasmin Solomon.

The 1985 Junior Forestry Judging team, eighth place. From left to right are Jared Holloway, Melissa Ryals, Naomi Holloway, and Daniel Holloway.

involved in the program throughout various clubs in the county. Swine projects have been a large part of Liberty County's 4-H programs, and the

117

county held many local swine shows. Youth also traveled to the North Florida Fair in Tallahassee and showcased their best pigs.

Liberty County is proud to be the 4-H home of Matt Schmarje, who had the honor of holding the position of the 1999–2000 State 4-H Council president.

Today, Liberty County features three major programs, including Forestry, 4-H, and Small Gardening and Landscaping.

The current agent in Liberty County is Monica L. Brinkley, who has held the position since 2002.

MADISON COUNTY
BY: DIANN DOUGLAS

Madison County Corn Club, 1916

Records show that Madison County 4-H began in the early 1900s. Extension agents worked with youth in corn and tomato clubs. In the early years, clubs existed in the school and 4-H'ers learned the

newest growing methods to produce better crops. Sewing was another early project mentioned in records.

In the 1930s and 1940s, clubs focused on growing and preserving food for the family. Home demonstration groups worked with youth to teach food preservation. Poultry and gardening projects were also popular. A newspaper article featured 4-H girls preparing a meal for the Board of County Commissioners using food they had produced from their poultry, garden, and orchard projects.

Madison County Swine Project, 1970s

Throughout the years, 4-H'ers participated in demonstrations and judging teams. Madison 4-H members participated in state fairs, district judging events, and public speaking contests. Over the decades, community clubs began to spring up with adult leadership from home demonstration volunteers. Old scrapbooks show pictures and reports from 4-H clubs in Pinetta,

Sunny Side, Sirmans, Cherry Lake, Enterprise, Greenville, and Hanson.

In 1940, sixteen youth attended the 4-H short course in Tallahassee. Girls reported participating in workshops on food preparation, food conservation, home improvement, leadership, news reporting, health, and clothing. The local newspaper reported the individual experiences of each attendee. Camille Brannan detailed her participation in the home improvement sessions and learned about home beautification, bees, dairy, and club organizations.

In the 1950s, a state-of-the-art agricultural center was constructed in Madison with a livestock show arena. Madison County Extension became the host of the North Florida Livestock Show and Sale. Participants of 4-H came from counties all across northern Florida to enter swine and steer. This show grew over the years and is still a popular event for 4-H'ers in five northern Florida counties.

119

Club work in the 1950s focused on swine, cattle, and row crops. One club had several beehives and sold honey as a fundraiser. Morris Steen remembers attending the National 4-H Congress in 1957, traveling with the Florida delegation to Chicago on a bus.

During the 1960s, Evita Miller recalls competing in district judging contests. Topics for judging included fabric and patterns and rating eggs for freshness. A bus trip to the Florida State Fair was always one of the big adventures for Madison 4-H'ers. This involved an overnight trip with opportunities for 4-H demonstrations, public speaking, and display of crops that were grown by youth.

Dolores Jones started her Extension career in Madison County in 1961, assigned to 4-H girls. Many of the clubs were held at schools, where

Madison County canning demonstration, 1960s

The 4-H/Tropicana Public Speaking contest

120

girls worked on clothing, food and nutrition, and home furnishings. Boys' clubs worked on livestock and farming projects.

Through the decades, project work continued to focus on livestock, food and nutrition, clothing, and citizenship. Youth participated at the North Florida Fair, district judging events, and summer camp at Cherry Lake. During the summers, senior 4-H'ers went to Legislature in Tallahassee and Congress in Gainesville.

Several 4-H school enrichment programs have become a tradition in Madison County. For seventeen years, 4-H Ecology Field Day brings all of the county third-graders to the North Florida Community College campus to learn how to be good stewards of the environment. The 4-H/Tropicana speech contest has been adopted into the Madison school curriculum for fourth, fifth, and sixth grade. It is not unusual when talking with

young adults that they remember the Tropicana speech contest as their first experience in public speaking.

Many 4-H'ers have been successful in their chosen professions and as leaders in the community. The list doesn't do justice, but those named are highlights from different decades: Monteen Cave, retired president of Bank of Madison; Evita Miller, retired from Ohio Extension, where she served as a state specialist in nutrition; Morris Steen, current president of North Florida Community College; and Alfred Martin, Madison County commissioner and fire chief for the City of Madison.

Madison 4-H continues to serve the youth of the community. Leadership and service to the community are strong values demonstrated as 4-H'ers learn by doing.

MANATEE COUNTY
BY: DIANA SMITH

The Manatee County 4-H Program is estimated to have begun in the 1920s with the late Ed Ayers, a county agricultural agent. Reports show that Manatee 4-H girls prepared grapefruit in a demonstration kitchen and a club member later received a scholarship to Florida State College for Women in 1931 (O'Berry 1989). The 4-H club was run through schools with a separate agent for boys and girls.

The Public Speaking Program began in 1952 in the classroom of Palm View Elementary teacher Inez Pettigrew. She saw the need for her students to develop public speaking skills and ran the program for several years at her school. In 1969, 4-H and Tropicana joined forces and began officially sponsoring the 4-H/Tropicana Public Speaking Program in Manatee County. In 1985, the program was expanded regionally, allowing students statewide to develop their public speaking skills. (Aalberg 1998).

In 1963, the decision to pull the 4-H program out of the schools led to a change that demanded volunteer support. Tom Greenawalt, an assistant agricultural agent at the time, was faced with the responsibility of recruiting volunteers to teach and work with youth directly through organized 4-H clubs.

In the summer of 1965, Greenawalt led 4-H'ers to assist with the Firefly Project in conjunction with NASA Goddard Space Flight Center in Maryland. The 4-H'ers and leaders combed local areas at night collecting fireflies, which were then frozen and sent to NASA as part of a Space Research Program (Greenawalt 2008).

These 4-H'ers are pictured with a 4-H welcome sign in Duette.

121

After nearly five years of meetings, the Manatee County 4-H Foundation was incorporated in 1970. In 1971, Louise R. Johnson established the Community Faith in Action 4-H Club, the first club for African-American children in Manatee County. The longest-running club in Manatee County, the Mighty 4-H'ers of Duette, was established in 1972 by Herb and Gwen Shuman. In 1974, Manatee County 4-H alumni Betty Glassburn took over the club and served as organizational leader for several years. During her leadership, the Mighty 4-H'ers of Duette established the Duette Fire Department, the first for a club in the state (Glassburn 2007). Glassburn also helped establish the Florida 4-H Volunteer Leader Forum in 1984, which is still in existence today. Today, the club is led by Glassburn's son Gene and his wife Jennifer, with thirty-four members. While the club is primarily a community club, members participate in projects

Inez Pettigrew's fifth-grade class, 1957 (Palm View Elementary School Archives)

including citizenship, community service, clothing construction, gardening, leisure arts, leadership, livestock, and photography.

In 1975, Deanna Summerfield was hired as the first 4-H agent in Manatee County, though agricultural agent Dr. Tom Greenawalt was called 4-H agent in 1963.

Residential camping has a long tradition in Manatee County. In 1957, Manatee County contributed to the development of 4-H Camp Cloverleaf. This commitment continues today as camp restoration, an annual community service project of the County Youth Council, and counselor trainings are held on-site at the camp. Having such a commitment to camping has allowed Manatee County to camp separately for the week. In 2007, during the fiftieth anniversary celebration of 4-H Camp Cloverleaf, Manatee County restored the same cabin it had built in 1957.

In addition to clubs, throughout the years Manatee County has offered a variety of special interest programs to 4-H youth, including land judging. In 2004, the senior Manatee County 4-H Land Judging team took first place at the state competition. This was a proud moment for team coach Travis Seawright, former Manatee County livestock agent, who had been coaching land judging teams for thirty-four years (Dymond 2004).

Distinguished 4-H alumni include Dr. Bob King, retired ophthalmologist (Banana Hill 4-H Club, 1944–1945); Brenda G. Rogers, County Extension director (Citizenship Washington Focus, 1974); Bill Galvano, Florida Legislature District 68 (Tropicana Public Speaking winner, 1976); and Lori Spivey, Third World Health Issues consultant (National Congress, 1992).

King (2002) states, "Participation in 4-H is one of the most beneficial and worthwhile experiences a youngster can have. 4-H teaches you to accept and fulfill responsibilities. 4-H teaches good citizenship."

Galvano (2008) shares, "It was an invaluable experience for me. The fundamentals I developed have stayed with me throughout my academic, professional, and political career."

These 4-H'ers salute the flag. Pictured from left to right are Jorad Holmes, Vincent Jeffries, Megan Cook, Jasmine Means, Veronica Freeman, and Michael Stephens. (Ted West photograph)

Virgil Best and Ronnie Albritton take a soil sample for land judging.

"I owe many of my accomplishments in college and now in my career to the early leadership and communication training 4-H provided to me," states Spivey (2008).

Through the years, the Manatee County 4-H Program has continued to reflect the ever-changing needs and interests of a diverse youth population.

MARION COUNTY
BY: ROSE MARZELLA

From humble beginnings, Marion County 4-H has a rich history as one of the first three counties to start a 4-H program in Florida in 1909. The earliest pictures date back to 1916, with the boys' pig and corn clubs. These specialty clubs operated through the public schools, as county clubs had not yet been established. They were the only 4-H programs available until the early 1940s, and the start of the girls' Sears Poultry Club. The Marion County Sears Poultry Show is now the longest continuously running poultry show in America. In 1946, at age fourteen, Leroy Baldwin showed his first 4-H steer at the Southeastern Fat Stock Show. Mr. Baldwin has since gone on to establish the Baldwin Angus Ranch, served as president of the American Angus Association in 2002, and his cattle are known the world over.

In 1964, the 4-H program left the schools and switched over to volunteers and county clubs. The same year, a local livestock show, the Southeastern Fat Stock Show, changed its twenty-year-old format and became the Southeastern Steer Show, requiring all exhibitors to be members of either 4-H or FFA. The Seminole Garden Project was first offered in Marion County in 1968, which allowed 4-H members to experience taking care of their own vegetable garden plot. Also in the early 1960s, Minnie Green started the Fairfield 4-H Club, which is now the longest-running club in Marion County. As members started joining from across Marion County, the name was changed to Indigo 4-H, and at its peak, the club had forty-five members.

In 1973, there were fourteen 4-H clubs throughout the county when Pat Hamilton retired as agent

Marion County 4-H Boys' Corn Club with twelve-foot-tall corn, June 16, 1916.

Marion County Girls' 4-H Club Poultry Show, sponsored by Sears. Ocala, Florida, 1945.

and Bob Renner, who remained for thirty years, and his assistant Debbie Ergle Jenkins took office. The new 4-H staff quickly re-established a 4-H presence in the school system with special interest programs and their Wheel Program, consisting of embryology, terrarium, and nutrition segments. At its peak, the Wheel Program was used in every elementary school in the county, with enrollment as high as 10,000 students, and 2,800 students in the embryology segment alone. The Southeastern Steer Show became the Southeastern Youth Fair (SEYF) in 1978, and is now the longest-running all-youth fair in the country without a carnival, and has the largest youth hog show in the state, with over 300 hogs shown every year. The SEYF also has over thirty other events from dog agility to creative foods, draws over 1,200 exhibitors, and attracts over 20,000 visitors.

Marion County has trained thirty judging teams that have won their respective national competitions, and 127 state-winning teams. To date, Marion County has held a twenty-seven-year winning streak for State Forestry Judging and has sent seventeen winning teams to National Horticulture Judging. It has sent 418 members to present their demonstrations at State Congress in Gainesville and has sent 131 members to National 4-H Congress in Chicago and Atlanta.

The Marion County 4-H Farm was founded in 1999 on a forty-five-acre lot southeast of Ocala to give suburban and urban 4-H members the chance to participate in large animal and other agricultural projects. Coordinator Nola Wilson has directed the construction of a steer barn, hog barn, classroom, and shooting sports shotgun range, and continues to oversee the operation and growth of this unique facility. During the summer, she uses the facility for her Safety Day Program for over 475 fourth-grade students, which hosts an average of eighteen learning stations focusing on safety in the students' daily lives.

By 2003, Marion County had forty-three community clubs, and in 2007, Agent Norma Samuel led a team including 4-H faculty, family and consumer science agents, and the Marion County Extension marketing and public relations specialist in developing the Munchy Adventures Program. This colorful magazine introduces youth ages eight to ten to simple, healthy lifestyle practices through fun and engaging activities. Several states have indicated interest in adopting the curriculum for statewide use in their 4-H programs, and Florida Ag in the Classroom requested that the team

develop a modified version of *Munchy Adventures* for the 2008–2009 third grade Ag in the Classroom curriculum.

Marion County has also claimed four winners of the state 4-H program's esteemed Partners in 4-H Award: Jimmy Glisson, Edsel Rowan, Leroy Baldwin, and Dave Baillie. The honor roll of Marion County 4-H graduates has included a FEMA agent, an administrator for the USDA, a state representative, cattle ranchers, community business leaders, and many more.

Hampshire Boys' Pig Club, September 2, 1916

MARTIN COUNTY
BY: LUCINDA HARRIS

The Martin County 4-H Program began in 1944 under the leadership of Levi Johnson. When 4-H first began in the county, there was more participation through school clubs than there is today. However, the main project areas remain the same with agriculture, home economics, government, and leadership still occupying the main focus of the program.

In the 1970s, two of the most successful programs were inspired by two grants received from *Reader's Digest*. The first was a Bicycle Safety Program for elementary and middle school students. This program consisted of one class plus a bicycle rodeo. "Rules of the Road" and other 4-H safety materials were reviewed and given to participants. The bicycle rodeo included bike inspections and special maneuvers and safety rules. Support from the community bike shops flowed in along with support from the sheriff's department. This project received a lot of media coverage during its existence.

The second was a Youth Citizenship Program for senior high school students. Participants in this program began their day with a pancake breakfast at 7:00 a.m and then participated in workshops. County commissioners were invited to the breakfast to meet the high school students that participated in this program. There were discussions on teenage decision-making concerning drugs, dating, and other confrontational subjects. Another year, youth got to voice their opinions to community leaders about the nuclear power plant on Hutchinson Island. This program continued for five to six years and added a lot of prestige to the Martin County Extension Program.

Currently, 4-H teens help plan and present a camp program for special needs teens in Martin County who are in high school. The program is led by the 4-H agent, adult volunteers, 4-H alumni, and teens. The camp is presented by teen counselors of Martin County 4-H.

Martin County 4-H Club, 1946

Camp Cloverleaf, 1961

MIAMI-DADE COUNTY
BY: TERESA SCHRODER

Miami-Dade County's Extension and 4-H programs didn't start until 1915, when Mrs. A. L. Monroe was hired as its first Canning Club agent. In those days, and several decades after, most girls grew crops of tomatoes, learned canning, cooking, sewing, and home décor. Just about all boys were involved in agricultural projects such as growing corn and raising hogs and cows.

One of our most renowned Miami-Dade County 4-H'ers, former Florida Governor (1978–1986) and Senator (1987–2005) Bob Graham, enjoyed dairy and beef 4-H projects in the late 1940s. His family owned and operated the Graham Dairy until 1962. He even has a heart valve transplanted (2004) from a Holstein cow (www.nndb.com/people/387/000029300).

When asked about his 4-H experience, Senator Graham stated, "Florida 4-H had a major impact on my life growing up in Dade County, Florida. I never forgot the lessons I learned on hard work and service to the community which continue to influence me today."

World War II and helping to feed America took precedent in the 1940s. Joan Nielsen, founder and editor of *SOCIAL*, Miami's premier society magazine for twenty-five years, said, "Although I didn't live on a farm, I unearthed a lot next door to grow a victory garden. My mom and dad were glad to have salads every day from my 'big dig.'"

She loved learning to cook and sew and even won a state award for her project (circa 1945). After

Pictured from left to right are: Ardee Coolidge, Rebekah Diaz, Joan Nielsen, Kathie Roberts, and Teresa Schroder.

hearing her speak, the station manager of WGBS radio called to ask if she'd like to do a teenage show on their station. Joan shares her story: "I said sure, and did that for a few years, and after awhile, Burdines sponsored us and I got $10 a show!—Big money back then. I don't mean this as bragging but 4-H was the push that I needed to go forward. I will do anything in the world for 4-H. It personifies the best in young womanhood."

The '50s saw the beginning of the Miami-Dade County Fair and Exposition and the hiring of our first African-American agent, Victoria Simpson. Walter Arnold, called "Mr. Youth Fair" by those who knew and loved him, took a small 4-H fair and turned it into one of the country's largest and most successful fairs. Today, close to 700,000 people come to the fair each year with 4-H participation reaching 1,200 exhibits and over 150

participants in the Fashion Revue, Share-the-Fun, demonstrations, and animal exhibits. The fair is still one of our best partners and is the largest event of the 4-H year.

Ms. Simpson, an Extension home economist, 4-H agent, and fair department head, made quite an impact on our program during her twenty-nine-year tenure with Dade County Extension and 4-H. She established homemaker and 4-H clubs with African-American families and the Miccosukee Indians, as well as establishing the homemaking department at the fair. The Dade County Youth Fair awarded her the Lifetime Award for more than forty years of distinguished service. Margaret Staples, Ms. Simpson's secretary, who was herself a 4-H'er in the late '50s, tells of her great appreciation and love for Ms. Simpson. "Ms. Simpson had a heart for everyone; she was a wonderful, compassionate,

Robert Graham judges at a 4-H event in Orlando, Florida, 1950.

Senator Robert "Bob" Graham

organized woman. She believed in preparing youth and enriching the lives of adults. She taught us character, to always give back to the community, and she was a strong advocate for higher learning."

Monica Dawkins, then 4-H/EFNEP agent, shares her memories of helping Ms. Simpson teach at the Native American reservations. "This was a time of transition for the Miccosukee. Many of the older generation were still living in traditional dwellings. Ms. Simpson brought new homemaking and cleaning skills, teaching them how to live in modern homes and sew modern clothes. I brought the EFNP Program to the children, exposing them to new foods and healthier eating habits." Although the Miccosukee did not continue the 4-H and Extension programs, they do have a large wellness center located on the reservation.

Miami-Dade County also established a large homemakers' program during this time that continued until recently. The wonderful women in these adult clubs, established and trained by the Extension agents, would then help the 4-H agents deliver homemaking programs to the youth. Through the years, they have helped a great deal not only by teaching but also fundraising to make it possible for underserved youth to attend Camp Cloverleaf.

In the 1960s and '70s, clubs became integrated both by gender and race and moved from after-school programs to members' homes. Kathie Roberts, current

4-H agent since 1996, remembers her mother, Audrey Hartman, had two clubs, one for boys and one for girls. When Kathie's brother became a teenager, Mrs. Hartman had to step down as the leader of her son's club. Women were not allowed to lead teenage boys.

Soon these antiquated ideas gave way. Kathie recalls, "In those days, teen girls looked forward to the county Fashion Revue where 4-H and FFA boys served as escorts for the models. Then in 1964, I was among seventeen participants from Miami who attended the first co-ed 4-H event held in Gainesville." This event, called The State Citizenship Conference, was later changed to State Congress. Mrs. Roberts remembers that her 4-H membership, from 1957 to 1965, "was a time of tremendous personal growth, from a very shy child to one that led county 4-H programs."

"Integration in Miami-Dade County was not easy; there was opposition," Mrs. Staples remembers, "but not as much as in other places." It was a good thing because it made more resources available to the African-American 4-H'ers. It was a challenging but good time." During this transition, Ms. Simpson reached out to all 4-H'ers. "She taught us to respect and appreciate everyone's culture."

In 1980, several of our most active and dedicated clubs were started. African Square 4-H Club, established in 1981, is Miami's longest-running 4-H Club. Monica Dawkins, 4-H/EFNP agent (from 1978 to present), remembers presenting the 4-H Nutrition Program to the park supervisor. Olinda Alexis, who began as an assistant to the park supervisor, became its leader three years later. She states, "I was so excited to be a part of 4-H. I thought 4-H was only for the country children and not for the city kids." Shirley Kelly, 4-H program assistant (from the mid-'80s to present),

transitioned the nutrition club into a traditional 4-H club. Shirley and Olinda have now assisted two generations in constructing garments and making accessories and home décor projects that are entered and modeled at the county fair. Ms. Alexis's members include her daughter, granddaughter, nieces, nephews, and a total of over fifty members annually. Ms. Alexis states that she is "like a big kid when it comes to 4-H Camp Cloverleaf." Her favorite activity is "sitting on the breeze-way at night looking at the stars (seldom seen in the city) and enjoying the quiet environment where only crickets and not city gun-fire is heard." For her members, she states, "Camp is like a well-earned vacation from home responsibilities like caring for younger siblings." Most of her members have never been out of the city and most have learned to swim and canoe during camp. In her twenty-seven-year experience with 4-H, the main difference and disappointment that she has observed is that fewer members remain in 4-H through high school graduation. "Many seem to lose interest once they get to middle school."

Two other very active and long-running clubs are Amelia Earhart 4-H, the remaining animal club, and Exciting 4-H, the first home-school club. Bobby and Sherry Gornto began Amelia Earhart 4-H Club in 1985. This club, which meets at Amelia Earhart Park, is very active at the fair and in competitions across the state. Students come to Amelia Earhart Park, where the animals are housed, on weekends and after school. They work very hard and have won several awards through the years.

Jan Prentice started the first Miami-Dade County 4-H Home-school Club in 1989. The 4-H method of "learn by doing" and hands-on projects were and continue to be a perfect fit with home-school educational philosophies. Jan shares some of her experiences and reasons for joining 4-H. "Our family was looking for activities to be involved in the community and be educational. We considered Scouting, but we wanted something the entire family could do. My husband had a wonderful experience in Florida 4-H so that seemed a good choice. In 1989, Ms. Shirley Kelly came and presented 4-H programs to several home-school families. Our first project was gardening at Amelia Earhart Park. The children blossomed with this approach. The club put in countless service hours, educated themselves, then taught others on many subjects and became aware of governmental issues, preparing them to be better citizens. Exciting 4-H members have expressed thankfulness for skills learned in 4-H and used in college and the workplace. I'm thankful for our 4-H agents and staff that help make the program so 'exciting.'"

No article about Miami-Dade County 4-H would be complete without mentioning Director Don Pybas. Mr. Pybas came to the county as a Sea Grant agent in 1978 and became director in 1997. Mr. Pybas has been and continues to be a great supporter not only of Extension but of 4-H, its members, volunteers, and staff. Patrick Prentice, a 4-H alumnus, remembers Mr. Pybas: "He was a great teacher and always had the time to teach us about marine science. He helped us learn about fish venting and assisted our efforts in teaching others." Mr. Pybas supported the 4-H'ers in their marine projects with opportunities, knowledge, and resources and is actively involved in our recently formed county fishing club, Rods and Reels 4-H.

The newest program the county has been involved in is Operation Military Kids. We have helped military support organizations bring fun programs to their Family Days and Hero Packs filled with items to encourage youth impacted by their parents' deployment. We are in the process of expanding

The Miami-Dade County senior team wins first prize at the 2007 Marine Ecology Judging Event. From left to right are: Eleanor Rodriguez-Rassi, Robert Otar, Rebekah Diaz, Lynette Herbert, and Karen Blyler.

this program in order to meet the needs of more military youth.

133

Slowly over the years the Miami-Dade County 4-H programs have changed from purely agricultural and home economics-based to those of great diversity. Its members, volunteers, and staff are engaged in: marine and environmental studies, Butterfly Wings, a seat belt safety competition, finance, government, public speaking, computers, leadership, shooting sports, fishing, exchange programs with Puerto Rico, and teaching at school science fairs. But this sophisticated world-class metropolis still has clubs that study the more traditional 4-H projects of sewing, cooking, nutrition, raising farm animals, horse judging, horseback riding, participation in the Homestead Rodeo Parade, and Camp Cloverleaf.

Although Miami-Dade County 4-H's focus has changed thoughout the years, its dedication to youth development has not. Students still find volunteers and staff whose goal is to see today's youth become tomorrow's leaders!

MONROE COUNTY
BY: DOUGLAS GREGORY

Monroe County's 4-H Program began in 1997, with Douglas Gregory as the first agent. Major programs within the county were marine environments and recycling. The longest-running club was the 4-H 4Him Club, which had run for eight years. In 2007, Monroe County 4-H made national headline news for their 4-H Staghorn Coral Restoration project. After only ten years, 4-H was forced out of the Extension Program in Monroe County due to county budget cuts.

Monroe County 4-H'ers with former 4-H Agent Kim Coldicott (front middle)

NASSAU COUNTY
BY: LeeANN AND NATALIE HUTCHINSON

Boyle, Bush, Carter, Coleman, Collingwood, Fulmer, Goodwin, Gressman, Hartsfield, Higginbotham, Hurst, Hutchinson, Johnson, Jones, Killmeyer, Owens, Page, Sawyer, Scott, Simmons, Smith, Tasso, Thomas, Williams, Zeorlin: these are just a few of the families who were and still are important to 4-H in Nassau County.

The 4-H club in Nassau County started around 1917. The first clubs in Nassau County were school clubs, held during school hours. The county agent led the boys, teaching them all things related to farming, and the home agent lead the girls' clubs, teaching the usual home-related subjects. The 4-H club was sponsored by the county commissioners.

The oldest living 4-H alumnus in Nassau County is Louise Owens Flood. Mrs. Flood was born in 1909.

She was one of nine children and six cousins all raised together, and all of whom were 4-H'ers. Mrs. Flood was one of the first 4-H'ers from Nassau County to attend the Washington, D.C., short course. It was her senior year in high school and there were just four 4-H'ers from Florida attending. Unheard of now, Mrs. Flood had to gain weight to participate—she was too thin! They rode a train to Washington, slept in tents outside of Washington, and had a wonderful time. Mrs. Flood later became a 4-H volunteer leader, and has influenced many 4-H members with her help, knowledge, and quiet dignity.

Gordon Ellis was the county agent in Nassau County for twenty-three years. He was interested in dairy farming and in training boys to be good dairy judges. Every Saturday, he would pick up a

135

Junior 4-H Fashion Show participants, 1973. From left to right are: Dolly Higginbotham, Kim Coleman, Tammy Crews, Louise Hurst, David Coleman, and Patty Conner. Sitting in the front are Vivi-Anne Anno and Vicki Nobles.

Above: Nassau County Bicentennial parade, 1976. The Nassau County 4-H Council participated with a float. The 4-H'er holding the American flag was Council President Ralph Hurst, Jr., and Dixie Fulmer, council vice president, was holding the 4-H flag. (Photo courtesy of Ralph Hurst, Jr.)

Left: First 4-H Horse Show at the Northeast Florida Fair in Callahan, Florida, 1967. (Photo courtesy of Gil Quarrier)

carload of boys, take them to a local dairy, and they would spend the day judging cattle. The dairy judging teams he trained did very well in state and even national events. Mr. Ellis was also excited about forestry. The 4-H boys' club had a tree farm with over fifty different tree species in it. The 4-H club members could identify just about any tree they found. They also had a Christmas tree farm, and used it to raise money for 4-H projects.

Judson Fulmer took over as county agent for Mr. Ellis in 1969 and brought a new direction to 4-H in Nassau County. Until then, the clubs were primarily school clubs, and were led exclusively by the county agent and home agent. Mr. Fulmer introduced the concept of volunteer leaders for the clubs, and for the clubs to meet at times other than just during school hours. Another change that took place was the combination of boys' and girls' clubs into local community clubs.

The oldest active club in Nassau County is the Callahan Country Kids. It was started in the early 1970s by Mattie Hurst and Betty Jo Higginbotham, but was called the Callahan Busy Beavers 4-H Club. As the members became older, being referred to as "busy beavers" became less popular, so the club changed its name to Callahan Country Kids.

In Nassau County, 4-H stayed mostly concerned with farming and home topics through the late '60s. Then the areas of citizenship, leadership, and other less farm- and home-related areas began to grow. Today, 4-H in Nassau County emphasizes community service, leadership, and citizenship. The 4-H'ers are encouraged to help others and to help themselves become better leaders and citizens. There are 4-H members involved in just about every 4-H project area and interest.

There have been many 4-H'ers from Nassau County attending the National Congress. They all

Town and Country 4-H Club's exhibit at the 1995 Northeast Florida Fair in Callahan, Florida. Pictured from left to right are: Randy Thomas, Martha Quarrier, Thomas Gill, Curtiss Quarrier, Doug Hodges III, Sabrina Hodges, and Robbie Thomas. The club won the Youth Beef Herdsman award that year. (Photo courtesy of LeeAnn Hutchinson)

have wonderful stories to tell, some of them quite amusing. Gil Quarrier remembers having lots of a new variety of grapefruit to give away. It was specially designed not to bruise. They put the theory to the test by rolling it down twenty-three flights of hotel stairs to see whether it would bruise or not.

When Nassau County 4-H'ers have finished with 4-H and gone on with the rest of their lives, 4-H has stayed a part of them, in one way or another. Skills learned in 4-H have helped them with college and careers. Many 4-H alumni have continued with 4-H by becoming volunteer leaders. Others have become Extension staff members. Many alumni have gone on to hold local and county-elected offices. Many serve on various service and community boards. There are Nassau County 4-H alumni in the medical field, teaching field, and business field. Many are entrepreneurs and small business owners. And yes, many have continued the honorable and proud profession of farmers

137

and ranchers. Yet, the real way 4-H has played a role in the lives of 4-H alumni is in how they interact with their communities afterward. Regardless of the career choice each has made, being active in the community is something that Nassau County 4-H'ers never forget.

OKALOOSA COUNTY
BY: LINDA MEYERS

Tracing back in our county's Extension history, the earliest county agriculture agent that we have record of was Mr. R. J. Hart, who served from 1917 to 1928. The home economics agent was Bertha Henry, who served from 1921 to 1930. We are unsure as to when the 4-H program actually started here, but we know that Camp Timpoochee, the first 4-H residential camp in the state, was established in Okaloosa County in 1926.

In the early years, the home economics agents had dual responsibilities and helped coordinate the 4-H Youth Program. Searching back, we found records of an active 4-H club program coordinated by Dora Stubblefield, home economics agent (1957 to 1961), followed by Ann Jeter (1961 to 1987), Charla Wambles (1967), and Marilee Mangrum Tankersley (1968 to 1974). Charla Wambles Cotton returned as the 4-H agent (1975 to 1982), followed by Elaine Courtney (1982 to 1988), Charlotte Turner (1989), Tammy Broxton Payne (1990 to 1992), Terry Henderson (1994 to 2000), and Jennifer Heady, who began with us as a part-time county employee in 2001 and became our full-time 4-H agent from 2003 to the present day.

Recollections from our past agents tell us that early community clubs met in the rural areas of

the county and were popular in Baker, Escambia Farms, Holt, and Laurel Hill. Boys' and girls' clubs met separately, with boys concentrating on agricultural projects that related to the family farm, and girls learning homemaking skills such

Club members learn the 4-H Pledge, 1969.

as cooking, sewing, and canning. Some of the early clubs were the Beaver Creek, Escambia Farms, and Blackwater boys' clubs, or the Merry Makers, Hopeful Homemakers, and Busy Bees for the girls.

138

Susan Forte, Florida's "Teacher in Space," meets with Okaloosa 4-H Council members, 1986.

In the 1950s, we found that the offices of the Extension Service were located in the basement of Okaloosa County Courthouse in Crestview, and that in the early 1960s, it moved to a new facility on Old Bethel Road, where we are still located today. At one time, the fairgrounds were located behind the Old Bethel Road facility, and to this day the storage room where the livestock were originally housed is called the "barn."

Ann Jeter remembers that Dora Stubblefield, who served before her, had a well-organized 4-H program. The agriculture and livestock agents also worked closely with the youth and had a very successful 4-H Livestock Program. Citizenship and leadership became a main focus of the 4-H program and many members served as club officers and junior leaders. Jeter recalled their having to rent a school bus to take all of the 4-H'ers from our county to Tallahassee for the short course each year (now known as Legislature). Our program continued to grow and evolve in the '60s and '70s. A 4-H County Council was formed, and in the 1970s, three senior 4-H'ers from our county—Beth Patten, Carol Walthall, and Robert Harden—went on to serve as officers on the 4-H State Council.

In 1975, several thousand Vietnamese refugees were living on Eglin Air Force Base. Okaloosa County 4-H worked with state 4-H specialists to organize programs involving recreation, crafts, and special interest projects to help with the refugees' problem of boredom and their need to become acquainted with American customs.

Clubs had grown all over the county, including in Baker, Laurel Hill, Fort Walton Beach, Crestview, Dorcas, Shalimar, Mary Esther, and Destin. The 4-H club wasn't just about cows, corn, and cooking any longer; the program now offered forty different 4-H projects. Children who were interested in environmental conservation, dog obedience, photography, and civic participation could easily find a community club to join. In the mid- to late '70s, there were as many as twenty active 4-H clubs, and membership grew from 150 members in the early '60s to 600 youth. In a *Playground Daily News* article written in the late 1970s, Dr. Ben Crawford, Extension horse specialist from the University of Florida, was quoted as saying, "In five years, Okaloosa County has gained some of the fastest-growing clubs in the state. Presently there are 600 members in 11 clubs. Over two-thirds of our kids are from an urban rather than a rural home."

Charla Cotton recalls that one of her most significant memories of the '70s was the development of the area horse program. This popular interest in our county continued to develop in the 1980s. Youth participated in judging teams, area and state horse shows, and horse camp. The Horse Advisory Committee sponsored adult horse camps and open horse shows as fundraisers to help support the Youth Program and maintain and improve the horse facilities at 4-H Camp Timpoochee.

The 1990s saw many changes. In 1991, sadness struck our county and the Extension Program

with the sudden passing of Charles Walthall, our director. In 1992, the County Extension facility was dedicated in memory of his twenty-four years of service, and the name was changed to the Charles M. Walthall Agriculture Center. Gerald Edmondson became our county director and continues in that position today.

In 1995, under the guidance and generous support of Fred Barber, the Okaloosa 4-H Foundation was established. The Foundation supports a $1,000 college scholarship that is awarded to an Okaloosa graduating senior 4-H'er. Fred Barber, who served as the agriculture agent from 1941 to 1951 in our county, had been a long-time supporter of the Florida 4-H program as well, sponsoring college scholarships and projects that continue to benefit many Florida youth today. Mr. Barber was honored as an inductee of the state 4-H Hall of Fame.

Teens learn how to buy a car at Money Adventures Day Camp, 2003.

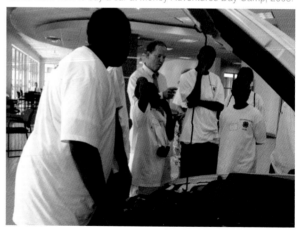

Also in 1995, Hurricane Opal hit the Panhandle with 115-mile-per-hour winds and fifteen-foot storm surge during our county fair. The devastation caused by this killer storm left a lasting impression on our 4-H'ers and club leaders. Many times they have held out a hand of support to other 4-H families and clubs who have unfortunately experienced a similar tragedy in our state.

In came 2000, and the 4-H program continues to evolve and change to accommodate the youth of today. The 4-H club welcomed youth ages five to seven years old in the program. More science and technology projects are developed to help youth with these growing fields of interest ranging from computers to robotics. The 4-H Honor Club takes the Health Rocks Program to schools in the community, and Money Adventures day camps teach teens good financial management skills. A unique partnership developed with the military and 4-H, and youth are able to participate in the 4-H program at U.S. military bases all over the world. Membership in youth programs on both Hurlburt Field and Eglin Air Force Base in Okaloosa County have continued to grow under the guidance of Jennifer Heady and now have over 300 members in after-school clubs. When asked about the importance of 4-H in Okaloosa County today, Heady said, "4-H continues to make a difference in the lives of our youth, helping to build strong character, learn life skills, and encourage a strong sense of community involvement."

OKEECHOBEE COUNTY

Agent Debbie Clements with Sharon Spann, Okeechobee County 4-H alumnus. Spann received the Walter B. Arnold Jr. Hall of Fame Award, July 2005.

More than 50 percent of Okeechobee County 4-H'ers live in a rural setting. In 2007, 6,198 youth enrolled in 7,948 4-H projects, and there were 246 clubs and 222 adult volunteers. Major projects in Okeechobee County are public speaking, beef, dairy, wildlife and fisheries, and consumer education.

141

Youth tend to their small animal projects at the Okeechobee County Youth Fair, 2005.

ORANGE COUNTY
BY: GLINDER S. STEPHENS AND
TIMOTHY A. PEHLKE II

Mrs. Nellie W. Taylor, who served as a home demonstration agent for nineteen years, started her career with Orange County 4-H on October 1, 1916. In 1920, she organized the County Federation of Women's Clubs, which included eight 4-H clubs. When 4-H first began, Mrs. Taylor worked only with girls, and the group was known as the "Canning Club." One-tenth of an acre was designated for a tomato garden. The girls grew the tomatoes and then canned them under her direction. Mrs. Taylor's greatest pleasure came from seeing "club girls" grow up and put what she taught them into practice. She was particularly proud that by 1935, she had six girls in 4-H clubs whose mothers were among the first 4-H club members. Her first visits to participants were in a horse and buggy. It was not until 1918 that the Board of County Commissioners assigned her a Model T Ford automobile to conduct Extension programs throughout the county.

Mrs. Taylor sought to include the boys in the gardening and poultry programs already available to girls. The boys' performances were admirable, and each year, one boy was awarded a trip to Gainesville to attend the boys' club short course. In 1926, Mr. K. C. Moore came to Orange County as the CED and assumed responsibility for boys' programs from Mrs. Taylor. At that time, there were approximately fifty boys enrolled in the program.

142

Betty Trevarthe, outstanding Orange County 4-H Club girl, works in her home garden, March 29, 1944.

The first 4-H club summer camp in Orange County was held at Rollins College during the summer of 1918. This camp was sponsored by the Women's Club of Winter Park and was attended by eighteen girls, with all expenses paid by the organization. One day during camp was set aside for Annual Visitor's Day, at which time the girls acted as hostesses to the county commissioners, county school board, presidents of women's clubs, the Chamber of Commerce secretary, and county residents who were interested in the girls' efforts.

In 1948, the Orange County Board of County Commissioners agreed to fund two new staff positions for Extension. One assistant county agent was assigned to the boys' program, while the other worked with the girls. These two new County Extension positions in Orange County

Boys State Lamp Contest, 1956. Kenneth Renne (left), from Pinellas, won first place. Fred Kast (right), from Orange, took second.

were the first new positions created in thirty-four years. Prior to this time, the county agent and home demonstration agent worked with adults and youth.

The 4-H clubs originated in Orange County in rural areas, with the agent teaching youth how to grow and can tomatoes. The agents also taught the youth life skills such as cooking, sewing, gardening, and caring for animals (such as cows, pigs, and poultry). Learning these skills helped families to live comfortably and secure more stable food supplies.

While 4-H'ers are still learning traditional life skills, they have broadened their interests and activities over the years. The population of Orange County has grown tremendously and today's youth are involved in hands-on projects that include rocketry, GPS mapping, public speaking, nutrition, robotics, and photography.

Some other facts that merit mention are:

• Terry Floyd had the longest unbroken tenure, working with 4-H for twenty-nine years. Terry worked with Orange County 4-H from 1972 to 2001.

• The longest-running club is The Ambassadors Public Speaking Club (now known as the Smooth Talkers), which has been around since 1983.

• County leaders inducted into the Florida Extension 4-H Hall of Fame include:

2002	Sarah and Dan Nichols
	Diane Shaw Anderson
	Henry Swanson
	Doris Base
	Terry Floyd
2006	Sandy Bekemeyer
	Fred Dietrich

• The 4-H Exploding Bacon Robotics Club placed third in the 2007 FIRST Robotics Competition held in Atlanta against an international field of competitors.

143

OSCEOLA COUNTY
BY: RENA AVANT AND TERI WILBER

Osceola County had its first fair between 1917 and 1921; the railroad offered free rides to anyone attending the fair. The still-popular baby show was held in the ladies' restroom. This early tradition opened up a great opportunity for Osceola County youth.

The 4-H club began in Osceola County around this same time. One of our first members, Ruth Yates (Spence), joined 4-H in 1928. Just two short years later, Ruth became the first member of Osceola County 4-H to be awarded a trip to National 4-H Congress. She earned this recognition by winning the State Home Improvement Project. National 4-H Congress was held in Chicago and Ruth was joined by five other 4-H'ers from the State of Florida.

In 1994, Ruth stated, "It was thirty years before the next Osceola County 4-H'er, Devo Heller, went to National 4-H Congress." Ruth's son Bill Spence attended National Congress in 1967, followed by her nephew Jim Yates in 1969.

June Gunn was Osceola County's first 4-H agent and was instrumental in building a solid 4-H foundation for the youth in our community. He was one of the early individuals that embraced the "learn by doing" motto. He continued as 4-H agent for twenty-five years until his retirement in 1954. During Mr. Gunn's time as agent, projects included dairy, citrus, and small engines for boys, and cooking, sewing, and citizenship for girls.

J. R. Gunn, D. L. Autrey, E. E. Hammond, and R. E. Elling with Surgo Champion, 1940

Milton "Bub" Bronson proudly shows a seventy-five-dollar check and blue ribbon received at the Osceola County 4-H Dairy Heifer Show, November 1952.

Jim Smith was the Osceola County agent from 1954 to 1981. He enjoyed taking the 4-H members to summer camp, which he ran while in college. He also taught all 4-H members to swim with the help of County Agent Marilyn Tileston. In 1950, eighteen Osceola 4-H boys headed off to Camp McQuarrie. During their stay, they participated in games, leadership events, and campfires.

Randy Yates with his demonstration, "Sign of Times," January 1972

From the late 1940s to the mid-1960s, Osceola County played a large part in the dairy community. Dairy exhibitors showed their animals on the cobblestone road in downtown Kissimmee. In 1952, Milton "Bub" Bronson won Grand Champion Dairy Heifer. This same year, the Kissimmee Valley Livestock Show (KVLS) built a new Agriculture Center, and it was considered the largest in the State of Florida. During the late 1960s, Osceola

County saw a transition from dairy cattle to beef cattle. The first steer show was held in 1967 in conjunction with the KVLS. This is still a tradition that continues during the annual fair held in February. At that time, the girls were not allowed to show livestock but participated in the Extension Homemakers Club. They used special green-and-white-striped fabric to construct their dresses to be worn at 4-H activities. They also learned many other skills that prepared them for all phases of family life.

In March 1968, Mr. Smith and Mrs. Tileston presented a sixty-foot demonstration at the Central Florida Fair showcasing Osceola's agriculture. The "Youth Building a Stronger America" exhibit won Best Exhibit. The population of 4-H continued to grow during the 1960s. Members of 4-H participated in the "Show Me Party," which is much like our county events. As a community service project, they raised money for the American Lung Association and tuberculosis.

Charles H. Bronson, current commissioner of agriculture for the State of Florida, participated in 4-H in the late 1950s and early 1960s. Bronson stated, "Young people can get only so much from textbooks. They need to explore new things and develop real life skills in order to gain self-esteem and become happy and productive citizens." Commissioner Bronson still continues to support the efforts of 4-H in Osceola County.

Silver Saddles, established in 1984, is the longest-running 4-H club in Osceola County. The first leaders of the club were Elaine Keir and Jane Trierweiler. Both leaders were very active in the horse program. Their success was shown through many awards, including state and national horse bowls and Horseman of the Year awards. Sue and Rob Carstensen still carry on the tradition of the

Members receiving the Proclamation for 4-H Week. From left to right, back: Karen Henry, Keenan Schmidt, Dalton Tupper, Jonathon Young, Ashley Avant, and Heather Young. Front: Lane Wilber and Brittany Avant.

Silver Saddles. Their son, Tyler, held many club offices as well as county and state offices. The members of Silver Saddles are very active in all aspects of 4-H, including horse, livestock, and community service programs.

Osceola County still has a strong 4-H community, with twenty-three community clubs and approximately 500 members. Many Osceola County members participate in projects from livestock to Fashion Revue. Osceola County Council participates in community service projects, district activities, and state activities.

PALM BEACH COUNTY
BY: MARTHA WEBSTER

In 1894, Henry Flagler discovered a primitive paradise on the eastern tip of the south Florida coast. Palm Beach was named for its spectacular palms and beaches and was first carved out as a county in 1909, taking its final and current shape in 1925. The early development was in part due to the Extension of the Florida East Coast Railway that brought workers for the grand Flagler Hotel and later tourists to the area. From the very beginning, Palm Beach County had the dichotomy of two economies—tourism on the coast and agriculture on the rich lands surrounding Lake Okeechobee, the second-largest inland freshwater lake in the continental United States.

The Smith Lever Act brought education from the land grant university system to the community. The establishment of the University of Florida Everglades Research & Education Center in Belle Glade in 1921 brought the land grant university to Palm Beach County. Expansion of the EREC and other Extension properties over the years came

Marvin Umphrey "Red" Mounts, agriculture missionary and farmer's best friend (Courtesy of M. M. Coulter)

148

through land donations made by George Morikami and financial donations by Wedgworth Farms, Inc. In 1925, when Palm Beach County had only one agent for the 1.3 million acres, Marvin "Red" Mounts was hired as the second agent. He was an extraordinary community educator who introduced and guided many youth to successful careers in agriculture. "Red" Mounts served for the next forty years, and the Palm Beach Extension Complex and Gardens are named for him. Dan Rousseau and George Wedgworth, president and CEO of the Sugar Cane Growers Cooperative of Florida, both attribute their successes to the influence of "Red" Mounts.

The 4-H club was taught by the agriculture Extension agents until the late 1950s, when professional agents were employed to work specifically with youth programs, educating them not only in agriculture but in family and life skills. In 1959, Marylou Shirar became the 4-H

agent in Palm Beach County. She hosted a local NBC program called *South Florida Almanac* that made it possible for the community to know more about 4-H. She worked to initiate the school enrichment program that continues to be a resource for teachers and an experiential learning

Palm Beach County 4-H Horticulture Clinic, 2003

opportunity for area students. She was creative in delivering special interest curriculum and in piloting university projects. During her time as 4-H agent, program assistants were added to support professional staff. The politics of the time reached out to challenge Marylou. Club integration became a force in determining youth club membership. Advisory Board minutes during this time reflect her efforts to meet the demands of current trends and litigation. Marylou's work and dedication was honored with her induction into the Florida 4-H Hall of Fame in 2002.

Palm Beach County also boasts the most devoted, active 4-H leader in the State of Florida, Helen Adler. For the past forty-eight years, Helen has been, and continues to be, the leader of the 4-H Helpful Hearts Club. Helen has led as many as three separate clubs at the same time. She has seen 4-H change from "cows and cooking" and was a master manager of volunteers. She organized her

Helen Adler, longtime 4-H leader in Palm Beach County

As family structures and youth learning demanded more expertise in the field of technology, 4-H met the challenge. In the twenty-first century, Palm Beach County youth members are discovering over 127 subject areas. Members are accepted in self-directed study, as well as clubs, so that senior-level youth can continue to participate in 4-H and meet the demands of multiple responsibilities outside the home. Youth continue to excel through 4-H education and recognition as national leaders and in international competitions such as nanotechnology.

clubs into groups of sewing, woodworking, food and nutrition, and recreation arts and crafts, each with an expert instructor. Marylou describes her as, "a devoted leader to children [with] a willingness to give. A leader before her children were 4-H age, during their 4-H years, and long after." Helen, too, was honored as an inductee into the Florida 4-H Hall of Fame in 2002.

There have been many dedicated agents and volunteers who have contributed to the development of Palm Beach County youth. "Red" Mounts, Marylou Shirar, and Helen Adler are exemplary of how 4-H has changed over the years to consistently and successfully prepare youth for life.

149

This Palm Beach County 4-H Club, Robomonkeys, competes at the 2007 International Robotics Competition in Atlanta, Georgia.

PASCO COUNTY
BY: JEAN HINK

Pasco County's 4-H Program began in 1909, when youth learned how to improve corn production. In that year, a teenage boy won the corn-growing contest. He was awarded a silver dollar for his high yield of corn. These early clubs were called corn clubs.

In 1912, Ms. Agnes Ellen Harris, Florida's first home demonstration agent, began the girls' tomato clubs. Pasco County was one of the original eleven counties that had tomato clubs. These corn clubs and tomato clubs later combined into the modern 4-H clubs.

The first annual report, "Florida Agricultural Extension Services," dated 1914 to 1915, listed Mr. R. T. Weaver as the demonstration agent and Miss Carrie Post as the home demonstration agent for Pasco.

In 1926, there were 993 4-H members, 225 of which participated in the "Grand March" in Dade City, Florida (Agent W. T. Nettles). In 1928, Pasco County girls attended a short course at the Florida State College for Women in Tallahassee.

Alice Storms, a Pasco 4-H member from 1938 to 1941, a second-generation 4-H'er, and a 4-H leader for twenty-four years, states, "4-H gave me a broad outlook as to what can be done in a community. I've seen young folks as a viable force…4-H has provided a rallying point for our family that has kept our family together. It has been a means of teaching children skills…providing leadership… and on top of all that, it's just been plain fun!"

In 1950, Mr. James Higgins, county agent (1940 to 1966), moved the Pasco Extension Office to the newly created fairgrounds, where the office remains to this day, making it one of the oldest, if not the oldest, continually operating Extension Offices in the state without having major renovations. Today, you can still see the names carved into the floor of the main meeting room of the original supporters. Many of the families involved in or supporting the 4-H program during this time are still involved today. Names such as Barthle, Herrmann, Boyett, Hall, and the Farm Bureau were original supporters.

The Progressive 4-H Club was started around 1954, and remains the oldest and longest-running 4-H club in the county. The club leader for the boys in 1954 was Frank Collura, and the agent in charge was James Smith. That year, five of the members from this club went on a field trip to the Ona Cattle Experiment Station for a day tour. Other activities held in 4-H that year were four ball games with other 4-H clubs, two chicken pileau suppers, two club floats that entered in parades, and two boys visiting other 4-H clubs to help in livestock judging.

In 1954, three boys from Pasco traveled to the Ocala Fat Stock Steer Show and Sale. Pasco Packing purchased Stuart Herring's steer for thirty-six cents per pound, and it was believed that G&W Grocery Company sold it in their store. Herman Schrader's steer sold for twenty-eight cents per pound and Leonard Steiert's went for twenty-nine cents per pound.

In 1954, Sears and Roebuck had a poultry plan. Ten Pasco 4-H boys received chicks (Bobby Backlini, Raymond Naeyaert, Henry Pike, Leonard Cimmadore, Robert Sessoms, Alva Cooper, Dale

The 1969 4-H club wins an award at the Pasco County Fair. From left to right are: Mike McCloud, Larry Barthle, Randy McCloud, Gerry Storch, Terry Schrader, Johnny McCarthy, Roney McCloud, Edward Storch, Ted Schrader, Bob Barthle, Gerry Schrader, and Steve Barthle.

The 1977 Pasco County Forest Ecology team

In 1964, the Progressive 4-H Boys Club and the Progressive 4-H Girls Club became a co-ed club. Charlotte Tomkow was one of the first leaders in this co-ed club. Her daughter, Lisa Hinton, is still an active supporter of 4-H, and members of the Tomkow family are still involved in 4-H.

According to Luther Rozar, assistant county agent from 1958 to 1966, "I have fond memories of 4-H." He tells a story about 4-H camp in 1962: "Chuck Smith and I were camping at a 4-H boys' camp and Hurricane Donna came through. We lost all our power and we couldn't do anything. I had given my car to the bus driver, who wasn't due back for a few days, and we had no way to get home. So, we hot-wired the bus and drove everyone to Ridge Manor where we finally found a phone that worked." Luther left Pasco County Extension and became the Extension director for Sarasota County. When he retired, he moved back to Pasco County and is a very strong supporter of 4-H.

Susan MacManus, a political science professor at the University of South Florida, was in 4-H for many years. Her mother, Elizabeth MacManus, was her 4-H leader. Susan said that 4-H gave her guidance as to what she could and could not do. "The fair and county events days were favorites. I found out I liked public speaking and if I had not learned about parliamentary procedure, I would be in a bad way today." She said her first trip to Washington, D.C., was when she was in 4-H. "Since then I have met four presidents, the first one being Lyndon Johnson. Patriotism, civic duty, and service to

Anderson, Stephen Bush, Mayo Karppe, and Chris Lee Craig). These boys had to "grow the birds out" and then in six months they had a show and sale.

In the late '50s and early '60s, Pasco County 4-H youth camped at Camp McQuarrie; there were separate camps for boys and girls. Youth were spotlighted and able to present their demonstrations and speeches on the new WEDU public television station. In 1964, Mary Lovelace did her first live television demonstration on how to make a flower arrangement.

151

country are important in 4-H. Fun and friendship also are a part of 4-H," she said.

In 1971, Jan Barthle, now Jan Dillard, sold her steer for seventy-six cents per pound. She later became the county's 4-H agent from 1976 to 1978.

In 1984, Pasco County's horse delegation brought back the coveted Golden Shovel Award from the state horse show (Chuck Cropp).

Pasco County placed First Place Team in the State Meat Judging Contest and First Place Team in the Retail Contest in 1997.

In 2008, Pasco County reached over 550 youth through club programming and 33,000 youth through school enrichment programs (Jean Hink, 4-H agent, 1998 to present).

Since its beginning, Pasco 4-H has increased and expanded its boundaries, growing from a strictly rural program to a dual rural-urban program.

The 4-H/Tropicana Public Speaking county contest, 2006. From left to right are Carson Brock, Kyle Van Buren, Mitchell Starr-Odajewski, and Lauren BoBak.

PINELLAS COUNTY
BY: VESTINA CRAYTON

Most who have had the privilege to be affiliated with 4-H through clubs, community events, or school activities would agree that 4-H is constantly evolving. Since the 1920s, Pinellas 4-H has achieved many successes. Below are some of the most notable milestones in the growth of Pinellas 4-H:

1920s AND '30s – TOMATO AND CORN CLUBS, THE FOUNDATION

In response to the economic times, home demonstration canning and sewing clubs were the first clubs to assemble. These clubs were the roots of 4-H youth development today.

Pinellas County Hen and Egg Show

1940s – CAMP CO-HO-DE ("CO-HO-DE" STANDS FOR COUNTY HOME DEMONSTRATION)

To ensure that the twelve 4-H clubs existing in Pinellas County maximized their 4-H experience, the County Home Demonstration Council purchased a

local vacation site from the Agricultural Chemical Association and named it Camp Co-Ho-De. Eighty-six-and-a-half-year-old Francis Gonzales recalls joining 4-H when the starting age was eight years old: "4-H built a solid foundation of skills that have carried me throughout my adult life. It gave me confidence, recordkeeping skills, and helped me foster lifelong friendships."

LATE 1960s – FIRST FULL-TIME 4-H PROFESSIONAL, ERNIE COWEN

Mr. Cowen recruited Pinellas County 4-H Agent Leah Hoopfer to attend a national 4-H agents meeting at Purdue University.

Pinellas County 4-H'ers

SINCE 1973 – SEMINOLE RIDERS, THE LONGEST-RUNNING CLUB

Inducted into the 4-H Hall of Fame in 2005, Mary Urquhart established the Seminole Riders in response to a growing interest in horses by her Girl Scout troop. Although she grew up with the love of horses around her, she wanted to provide her troop with researched-based information about the development, growth, and maintenance of horses. She turned to 4-H. "I knew I could get quality information from 4-H," said Urquhart. For their community service project, in partnership with the Kiwanis Club, the Seminole Riders created Horses for the Handicapped. Members of the club are trained in the three roles of horse handler, side walker, and loader. This knowledge gives the students the skills required to assist disabled youth with riding and appreciating horses. As she reflects and lovingly looks at the place where the Seminole Riders still meet today, she refers to the barn as "The Barn of Smiles."

LATE 1970s AND EARLY 80s – THE EXPANSION OF AGRICULTURE PROGRAMS TO INCLUDE MORE URBAN PROGRAMS

Agents Shirley Bond and Nan Jensen were the pioneers that facilitated the expansion of the Pinellas County 4-H Program by adding projects such as energy and water conservation, ecology, and recycling, all of which address the needs of an urban community. It was during this time that 4-H began to foster partnerships with other youth service organizations. By utilizing a more collaborative approach, Bond and Jensen secured a substantial federal grant that added twenty-six program assistants to the 4-H program. The additional staff enabled the duo to be instrumental in organizing the "latchkey" program by offering educational summer camp programs and operating a mobile classroom that offered nutrition and ecology classes. Eighty-five-year-old Kathleen Anthony of Largo fondly recalls her days as one of the twenty-six program assistants and her own children's involvement in 4-H. "I have great memories of 4-H. The experiences taught me how to interact with others and how to compete. If you don't compete you don't get better."

LATE 1980s – EMBRYOLOGY WAS INTRODUCED INTO THE CLASSROOM

This learning experience teaches students about the embryonic development of a chick through the hatching process. Betty Lipe, 4-H educational instructor, reflects on why this program is important and why it continues to receive seventy-five to one hundred requests each year from teachers. "This project is one of the ways to help kids understand where their food comes from. Living in an urban county, kids do not get to experience life cycles like kids in a rural community."

The 4-H horse project teaches youth sportsmanship and horsemanship. Here, a young 4-H'er shows her horse in a showmanship class. Tampa, Florida.

1990s – INTRODUCTION OF YOUTHMAPPING

As part of a research project on collaboration, three national organizations—the Center for Youth Development and Policy Research, the National 4-H Council, and the National Network for Youth—brought the Community YouthMapping process to Pinellas County. Pinellas County youth took the responsibility of collaborating with the community to survey, collect, and analyze data; create youth/adult partnerships; and promote community awareness on the opportunities available to youth

These 4-H'ers participate in a toy drive for Operation Military Kids, a special program within 4-H.

and their families to enhance their ability to establish and maintain a healthy, positive environment for all citizens (Pinellas County YouthMapping, *Bridging Our Vision with Experience Report*, page 3–4).

1991 – THE OCHS 4-H EDUCATIONAL CENTER OPENS

The Ochs Center provides urban youth the opportunity to develop agriculture awareness along with the skills needed to successfully maintain a vegetable garden. The Center also focuses on the conservation of natural resources and sustainable life choices.

LATE 1990s – 4-H IN THE CLASSROOM, PIZZA GARDEN

Pizza Garden is an agriculture adventure that teaches youth about where their food comes from by using something that children love to eat…PIZZA!

2004 – 4-H AFTER-SCHOOL, PARTNERSHIP WITH THE YMCA OF SUNCOAST ESTABLISHED

The 4-H After-school Program is a fun, educational, hands-on experience for youth ages eight to twelve to learn life skills through programs in the area of nutrition. Youth meet in a small group once a week for an hour and a half with a volunteer leader or an after-school staff person who received training and mentoring from the 4-H program staff (*Three-Year Strategic Plan*, page 9).

2005 – OPERATION MILITARY KIDS (OMK)

OMK is a program that reaches out to military youth and families before, during, and after their parent(s) are deployed. The Tampa Bay Program is a partnership between Hillsborough and Pinellas County 4-H (*Three-Year Strategic Plan*, page 8).

2007 – 4-H FAMILY DEVELOPED AND IMPLEMENTED

This unique type of programming provides an opportunity for youth and adults to learn together in order to help create safe, positive, and supportive environments that will allow family members to thrive and develop (*Three-Year Strategic Plan*, page 24).

Pinellas County 4-H has come a long way since tomato, corn, and sewing clubs. Today, youth can select from over 150 projects to learn important life skills. Former 4-H Agent Shirley Bond says, "4-H is about teaching kids, with the help of our adult volunteers, how to identify a problem, and go through the process to come up with a solution." Group leader and former child 4-H'er Tonya Poruba says, "4-H continues to teach students about deadlines, discipline, and time management." Through the decades, Pinellas County 4-H has adapted and embraced the growing needs of a unique and diverse community by creating innovative programming for our youth.

Asian Neighborhood Family Center 4-H Club

156

POLK COUNTY
BY: NICOLE WALKER

Polk County first sent youth to camp in Wimauma in 1920 (Cooper, page 70). Much of what is currently known about Polk County 4-H was related through Mr. Arthur Bissett, who passed in the fall of 2007 in his early nineties. School-based clubs were pioneered in the 1940s by Mr. Bissett, who served as the assistant county agent.

Photos and news articles have been located in the Extension office, dating back to 1937. In those days, there was no mention of a "4-H agent" as we know them today; instead, the home demonstration agent, Ms. Lois Godbey, played a major role in the education of 4-H club members, mainly girls.

Girls attended Camp Miller, located near Haines City, which was built in 1922 by the Polk County

Federation of Women's Clubs. Interestingly, a health and nutrition camp was begun at Camp Miller. It was reported that one year, girls were sent with the goal of *gaining* weight for better health, a very different perspective from today's concerns about youth obesity, and reality shows such as *The Biggest Loser*.

The Polk County Youth Fair began in 1947 and has had a tremendous and positive impact on the countywide program. The 4-H members were heavily involved in dairy and home economics projects in the early days.

In 1939, Ms. Godbey reported that 790 girls between the ages of ten and sixteen were enrolled in the program. Today, Polk County consistently

U.S. Representative Adam Putnam, a Polk County 4-H alumnus

Polk County Dairy Judging team, 1980, pictured with dairy magnate T. G. Lee (third from left) and John Brenneman, dairy agent (second from right).

ranks among the top five counties in the state with the highest number of community-based clubs. Youth also participate in school enrichment, after-school clubs, day camps, and residential day camping at the 4-H Camp Ocala center. There are two full-time 4-H agent positions, now held by William Hill, Jr., an Extension veteran since 1985, and Nicole Walker, 4-H agent since 2000. Influential 4-H agents included Alice P. Kersey, a thirty-three-year Extension agent; John Brenneman, born and raised in Polk County and an agent for thirty-two years; and Ruth Ann Miller.

Polk's greatest and strongest heritage has been in community-based clubs. Groups that existed for at least twenty years include the Belles and Boys 4-H Club of South Lakeland and the Amigos 4-H Club, Actioneers 4-H Club, and Home Grown 4-H Club of North Lakeland. The Imperial 4-H Club of Bartow also has a long history of successful club work.

The most popular projects today include swine, cattle, shooting sports, marine science, community service, and foods.

When the Florida 4-H Hall of Fame was established in 2002, several Polk County citizens were inducted

Home Demonstration Agent Lois Godbey

in the first class, including the Honorable Adam Putnam, a U.S. Congressman from Florida, who was a 4-H member and active participant in the Polk County Youth Fair and the 4-H Legislature Program. Other inductees include Mr. Arthur Bissett, 2002, and Mr. Max Hammond, 2004, a long-time cattle and citrus grower, who was an early supporter of the Polk County 4-H Foundation.

PUTNAM COUNTY
BY: BOBBI WATSON

Putnam County 4-H has been around since at least 1913, with Mr. T. E. Waldrup (field agent of the Southern Railway in farm improvement work) frequently assisting. The first clubs were the Boys' Corn Club and the Girls' Canning Club. The first club to actually include 4-H in its name was the Putnam County 4-H Club, with Mr. Tommy Clay, Sr. serving as the leader. Through the years, there have been several programs of interest. These programs have progressed from corn-growing and canning to livestock projects. Currently, the major programs are embryology and poultry with 123 members and swine production with sixty-nine members.

Over the years, there have been several general clubs and a few specialty clubs. As with most programs, Putnam County had clubs fold at times

few times, along with leaders, but they've always met in Satsuma, Florida. The founding leader of Kountry Kids was Kathy Seihler. She was the leader from 1988 until 2005. Other leaders over the years have been Sally Jacob, who co-led with

Hog 'n' Ham participant. The Hog 'n' Ham project teaches youth about the process in which livestock is processed into edible cuts of meat.

Horticulture Judging and Identification Contest

and others were simply handed over to other leaders. Of the twelve current clubs, Kountry Kids is the longest-running and going strong at twenty years. The actual meeting place has changed a

Kathy until 2005; Mary Ann Bridges, who co-led with Kathy by leading the juniors from 1988 until 2005; and Pam Buchanan, who led the cloverbuds for a few years. During this time, club enrollment ranged from twenty to forty members. In 2005, Mandy Guthrie took over the club and is the leader presently. Projects over the years included Tasty Tid-bits, swine production, beef production, and embryology. They have also participated in three County Fair Club Booth competitions.

Putnam County has had some distinguished 4-H alumni over the years, including Hermon Somers, who is currently serving as a county commissioner in Putnam County. Of our current leaders, two of them are alumni of Putnam County 4-H. As a member, Traycie Shrouder Tilton participated in livestock shows at the County Fair and other projects. She has been serving as leader of the Agri-Explorers 4-H Club in Hollister since 2004. As a leader, she has assisted youth with livestock projects and other areas of interest to them.

Bobbi Jean Watson was a member of the Little Gold Nuggets 4-H Club, which changed its name to Silver Lake Shooting Stars 4-H from 1996 until 1998, when the club folded. In 1998, she joined the newly established Bostwick Bronco Ropers 4-H Club, where she stayed until 2001 when she graduated. While in these clubs, she participated in the rabbit, swine production, and beef production projects. She also participated in Consumer Choice, livestock judging, Camp Ocala as a counselor, Congress, Legislature, Citizenship Washington Focus, and Community Pride. From 2001 until 2003, Bobbi served as an adult volunteer for the Putnam County 4-H Program, and in 2003, became a co-leader of her alma mater club, the Bostwick Bronco Ropers. As a leader, she has assisted youth with projects in their field of interest, established a care and concern in the members for their community through the Community Pride

Proposal Project, and challenged them to take every opportunity that 4-H has to offer them.

Some significant events have occurred over the life of Putnam County 4-H. On November 15, 1913, the first Farmers' Convention was held, which allowed funds to be appropriated for the corn and canning clubs. In 1953, the Putnam County

Putnam County Farmers' Convention. Palatka, Florida, November 15, 1913.

159

4-H Livestock Judging team participated at the State Competition. In 2000–2001, Putnam County 4-H held the Special Kids Rodeo, which allowed the county to extend the opportunities of 4-H to handicapped children as well as expose them to some aspects of agriculture they might otherwise have missed. In 2002, Putnam County had an Exchange Program, which allowed the members of Florida to see what other 4-H members do in other states.

SANTA ROSA COUNTY
BY: ANGELA QUALLS

From a simple agrarian past to a high-yield and high-tech future, Santa Rosa County 4-H programs have kept in step with the evolution of business and life in the county. Early 4-H visionaries saw that the best way to infuse newly gained scientific knowledge into the time-honored and trusted agricultural practices of the early 1900s was by allowing the youth to experiment with the new methods and technology. Using the positive, inquisitive, and competitive nature of youth, 4-H helped blend classroom science with tried-and-true farming methods. Farming is still important to Santa Rosa County, but the county has added many more industries since the 1900s and 4-H continues to provide youth the practical skills and knowledge they will need to succeed.

Corn clubs for boys and tomato clubs for girls were the very beginning of Santa Rosa County 4-H. L. N. Findley of Jay was one of the first corn club boys. He made one of the first trips for boys to the National Corn Exposition held in Columbia, South Carolina, in 1912. He attended with an Alabama delegation led by Director L. N. Duncan.

A. L. Johnson of Milton attended club camp at Floridatown and attended a week of club work in Gainesville with Agent Hudson. Other corn club members were Rusty Grundin, Osceola Simmons, Raymond Simmons, Frank Simmons, and Walker Simmons. Rusty Grundin suggested the name for Camp Timpoochee in 1932. Some of the original tomato club girls were: Mrs. Agnes Beal and Mrs. Elmer Hawsey of Jay, Miss Ruby Robinson and Miss

160

John Woodruff of Santa Rosa County won the State Tractor Operators' Contest and represented Florida at the Eastern States Tractor Operators' Contest in Richmond, 1957.

Above: Albert Jones with some of his prize-winning and money-making poultry. White Rocks, Milton, Florida.

Below: Fallout shelter in Jay, Florida, July 10, 1964. (Photo by Hilton T. Meadows)

Verlie Robinson of Wallace, Mrs. Wiley Williams and Miss Lora Botts of Milton, Mrs. Albert Golden of Bagdad, and Mrs. R. H. Broxson of Holley. There have been many 4-H agents throughout the years who have always encouraged youth to become better citizens.

Today's 4-H program mission is to "create supportive environments for diverse youth and adults to reach their fullest potential." Santa Rosa County Coordinator Vickie Mullins and Program Assistant Angela Qualls present opportunities given by the land grant university system, USDA, other governmental grants and community professionals for the youth of Santa Rosa County to "learn by doing" and serve "by learning." Although 4-H is still concerned with passing on the best agricultural and domestic practices, it also provides youth with opportunities to: 1) take active leadership roles in the legislative and judicial system of our county through Teen Court and county commissioners' meetings (4-H youth have led the charge in several community

initiatives and made several presentations to county commissioners); 2) work effectively with emergency responders following Hurricane Ivan and through starting a 4-H TEEN CERT Program; and 3) become effective managers in tomorrow's business world through learning leadership skills as youth leaders. In 2006–2007, over 4,000 youth have been involved in 4-H work. The majority of these have participated in school enrichment programs: 4-H/Tropicana Public Speaking, Farm Tours, Marine Ecology Field Days, and after-school programs. Santa Rosa County currently has nineteen clubs working on a variety of projects, from traditional animal projects to science and technology. Since 2006, Santa Rosa 4-H'ers have embarked on a campaign to teach other youth about healthy lifestyle choices in response to the growing childhood obesity epidemic. Santa Rosa County may not have the largest number of youth, but we have 4-H members who make a difference in their community today and will definitely make a difference in the future.

SARASOTA COUNTY
BY: MARCIA MORRIS

In Sarasota County, 4-H club work began through Manatee County in the early days of Extension, as Sarasota County was originally part of Manatee County. The first agents in Manatee were U. C. Zeluff and Eloise McGriff in 1916. The first agent for the newly created Sarasota County was P. M. Childers in 1927. The first agents to work with 4-H youth were the agriculture and home demonstration agents, W. E. Evans and Sara Horton. The first full-time 4-H agent appointed was Elva Farrell in 1976.

The 4-H office was located in the county courthouse basement, where many Extension programs and

classes took place. Many clubs were organized in schools and homes as volunteer leaders were recruited. Livestock, food preservation and preparation, sewing, poultry, and dairy were popular projects until the late 1990s. Livestock, arts and crafts, horse, marine science, and public speaking are the most popular projects today. The county fair remains a strong focus for county 4-H members, with a large livestock and arts and crafts participation every year.

Sarasota County has several long-running clubs. The Livestock Club has been continuous for over fifty-five years. Charlie Vann and his late wife,

These 4-H girls learn home economics during a club meeting.

Evalena, had served as the club leaders of the club for thirty years. The club focus is on livestock projects, and over the years, the Vann's farm has served as the host for numerous steer and swine projects for many area youth. Mrs. Vann was a strong supporter of the Citizenship Washington Focus Program and served as a chaperone for many years. Another long-running club in Sarasota County is the Ridin' Rednecks 4-H Club, which started in 1967 under the leadership of Don and Marlene Strickland. Both Don and Marlene have been recognized as Leaders of the Year by the state 4-H program. The club started as a horse club but later turned its focus to livestock and other projects. The longest-serving 4-H leader is the late Carl Bixler, who served over forty years as

a leader. Enrollment in 4-H has remained steady over the years.

The most distinguished 4-H alumnus from the county is Lisa Carlton, who was a member of the Ridin' Rednecks and currently serves as a state senator. Sarasota 4-H is heavily involved in community service and youth leadership development. Many Sarasota youth have been active in district and state leadership programs and judging teams. Summer camping is probably the most popular 4-H event in Sarasota County, filling up Camp Cloverleaf each summer.

The 4-H staff expanded to two full-time agents in 1978. Current staff in 2008 includes two 4-H agents, Marcia Morris and Keith Wilson; a 4-H program

State Girls' 4-H Club Council officers, 1950–1951. First row: Tally Coleman, Sarasota County, vice-president; Sallie Wilson, Madison, president; and Wylene Mayfield, Volusia, historian. Second row: Jackie Cummings, Lake, assistant secretary; Barbara Jean Dame, Broward, secretary; and Gay Roberts, Hardee, treasurer.

Enjoying a canoe ride at Camp Cloverleaf, 2007. From left to right are Wayne Dahlberg, Sean Russell, and Jamie Bland.

assistant, Sheila Holland; and a 4-H administrative coordinator, Barbara Lechky.

Currently, there are thirty-eight 4-H clubs with 700 members and 3,500 school enrichment members who participate in public speaking and radish-growing projects.

Other significant events in Sarasota County 4-H include:

- 75 years ago: The Sarasota County Fair started, offering 4-H club members the opportunity to display project work and participate in shows and exhibits.

- 50 years ago: 4-H Camp Cloverleaf was built. The camp would provide the camp experience to hundreds of Sarasota County 4-H members for the next fifty years and remains the most popular destination for members every summer.

- 35 years ago: The Sarasota County 4-H Foundation was established. This group has provided financial support to county members annually and serves as a key support group for county programs.

- 25 years ago: The 4-H Radish Growing Contest was started in Sarasota County for third-grade students and continues to remain a popular program in local schools.

- Most current event: County Events Day and the Sarasota County Fair.

165

SEMINOLE COUNTY
BY: GABRIELLE SAMUELS

The Seminole County 4-H Program is fortunate to have such a rich and extensive history. The first Extension agent in Seminole County was the home demonstration agent, Mozelle Durant, who served from 1914 to 1915. The first County Extension director was Charles Berry, who served from 1915 to 1918. Barbara Hughes became the seventh County Extension director and the first female to hold this position in 1993. The first full-time 4-H agent, Shelda Wilkens, was not hired in Seminole County until 1984.

Gabrielle Samuels, a member of the Sonshine 4-H Club, and Shelda Wilkens, 4-H agent, after a successful baking session.

In 1972, the Sanford Mighty Clovers 4-H Club was founded by Mrs. Linda Bose. Club projects included woodworking, gardening, aeronautics, cooking, and baking. Annual camping trips were part of the club's calendar of activities. The location of these trips included the University of Alaska and the Yellowstone National Park. Ecological preservation was one focus of community service projects.

The "Hoofing It" Horse 4-H Club was founded in the early 1990s by Mr. and Mrs. Ibert Isaacson, active 4-H volunteers for over twenty-five years. Members have competed in horse shows at the county, district, state, and regional levels. As a community service project, members provide an annual open horse show for disabled equestrians. Members participate in all aspects of horsemanship: competition, training, and basic horse care. Primary club leadership is now provided by Elizabeth Isaacson-Jett.

These 4-H club members give a demonstration on how to extract honey from the comb at the Central Florida Fair in Orlando, Florida.

The Sonshine 4-H Club was started in 1990, the first club for homeschoolers. It was founded by Mr. and Mrs. Phil and Kathy Robertson and Mrs. Susan Davis. Projects included Discovering 4-H, sewing, cooking, and baking. In 1996, the club began volunteering at the Sanford Zoological Park; this community service project was facilitated by Steve Decresi.

Seminole County has participated in numerous team competitions on state and national levels. They participated in the first state Horse Bowl contest in 1985. Seminole teams have gone on to be state champions in forestry, wildlife identification, Horse Bowl, and LifeSmarts. LifeSmarts is a contest sponsored by the National Consumer League to educate youth. In 2003, they were named national champions.

With the assistance of adult helpers, 4-H'ers Francine Huggins (left) and Christina Bukey (right) display items made for a community service project. Both girls also served as County Council presidents during their time with 4-H.

The Teens In Action Club is dedicated to serving the community. Youth and 4-H volunteers cooperate to complete service projects. Teen Club and Clover Kids are also clubs dedicated to service. Teen Club members provide leadership and guidance for Clover Kids throughout the completion of 4-H and service projects. This concept of club cooperation is unique to Seminole County.

The following individuals are among the distinguished members of our Seminole County 4-H community. Both Mr. and Mrs. Ed Yarborough were ardent supporters of 4-H, contributing time and resources to the Seminole County 4-H Program, and they were also community leaders. The Yarborough Family Ranch has been elevated to the Agricultural Hall of Fame.

Shane Michael was a member of the Canter-lope Chaos 4-H Club; he joined the Horse Program in 1997. After graduating from the 4-H program, he returned in 2006 as a 4-H agent. As the second 4-H agent in Seminole County, he oversees the Horse Program.

County Council President George Nunnery, Jr. was featured in several local newspapers. Cooking skills gained from the 4-H program earned him publicity. In a generous gesture, he catered for Home Economics Agent Barbara Hughes' wedding. Nunnery was also on the district committee responsible for planning the first Junior Congress Program in Florida. He is a graduate of Johnson & Wales culinary school.

Charles Gambaro represented Florida 4-H youth at the National 4-H Conference. From 1995 to 1997, Gambaro served as Seminole County Council president and was also Florida State 4-H vice-president. He is now a school board member in Flagler County.

Seminole County 4-H alumni have went on to become police officers, 4-H agents, teachers, missionaries, chefs, homemakers, and breadwinners, among others.

167

SEMINOLE TRIBE OF FLORIDA
BY: MICHAEL BOND

The Seminole Tribe of Florida 4-H has come a long way, dating back to 1955 and first known as Seminole Indian 4-H. Some of the earliest programs were chicken projects and cooking and sewing classes for both boys and girls. The agents assigned were considered "Special Indian Agents." The first Extension 4-H agents were Mr. Fred Montsdeoca and Mrs. Edith Boehmer. Fred

The Seminole youth attended Camp Cloverleaf, and the first year's group is still talked about today! "An incident took place during the first camp attended that was long remembered and talked about. Soon after the boys arrived at the camp, all of them disappeared. A frantic search of the camp premises and surrounding area was fruitless. Finally, someone looked out on Lake Frances,

Seminole boys and girls dig and can some ornamental plants to take home from their first 4-H camp at Camp Cloverleaf. From left to right: Elise Johns, Lawana Osceola, Connie Johns, Richard Smith, Jesse Osceola, Joe Norton, Nellie Smith, Elise Tommie, Augustina Gopher, and Rosie Billie.

worked with the young men while Edith worked with the young women. The boys were the first to get involved with 4-H, showing a strong interest in beef cattle. The first projects were cattle judging teams, which competed at county, district, and state competitions. Mrs. Boehmer worked closely with the girls in areas of home economics and gardening. In the early days, Seminole boys thought that tending to gardens and crops was the responsibility of women (Watkins, M. O. 1976).

on which the camp was located, and spotted swimmers playing almost a half-mile out from shore. A boat trip out to the swimmers revealed them to be the missing Indian boys. The boys were excellent swimmers, having grown up in the swamps and along the canals of the Everglades and thought nothing of swimming that distance." (Watkins, M. O. 1976)

Mr. Montsdeoca resigned in 1966 and Glenn Lovelace took over the program from 1967 to

1969, followed by Jack E. Bass from 1967 to 1973. After Mrs. Boehmer, Mrs. Fulton worked with Seminole women from 1958 to 1968, followed by Connie G. Kilbrew from 1969 to 1970 and Vicki Chipman from 1970 to 1972. In 1974, the Special Indian Agent Program was discontinued and the reservations had to work with Extension personnel from the counties in which they resided (Watkins, M. O. 1976). Between 1974 and 1992, there is no literature describing Seminole Indian 4-H. What is known is that tribal members Allen Huff and Mary Jean Koenes were 4-H leaders and conducted mostly animal projects.

In 1992, the Special Indian Agent Program was reestablished through the U.S. Farm Bill. Funding was made available for a special program known as the "Extension Indian Reservation Program (EIRP)." At this time, the Seminole Indian Tribe became a "county" for administrative purposes, and therefore was assigned their own Extension professional. At the same time, the Seminole Tribe appointed tribal member Polly Osceola-Hayes as the 4-H coordinator for the tribe, and projects and the curriculum "took off." The Seminole Tribe of Florida has six reservations; Brighton, Big Cypress, Immokalee, Hollywood, Tampa, and Fort Pierce. In 2006, the special "Indian" programs became known as the "Federally Recognized Tribe Extension Program (FRTEP)." The current Extension educator is Michael Bond, who came on board in 2004.

Today, Seminole Indian 4-H is one of the most successful programs in "Indian Country." The Seminole Tribe has traditionally been an agricultural and animal husbandry community. Approximately 50 percent of youth and young adults are introduced to these histories through 4-H school enrichment programs. These school enrichment programs are tied in with Florida's

The Seminole Tribe, Inc. supports Florida 4-H in many ways. They have been the signature sponsor for the annual golf tournament for the past two years. 2007.

Master Naturalist and Florida Master Gardener curriculum. Partnerships also involve further hands-on education with Florida Farm Bureau. Also, new programs are being introduced, such as the NASA Space and Robotics Curriculum.

Three of the six reservations are involved with gardening projects including both boys and girls. It is through these programs that members are exposed to recordkeeping and financial responsibility. Today, the youth are still participating at local, regional, and state-level competitions. In 2007, proposed by the Seminole Indian Tribe 4-H, a consortium of Southeastern Native American 4-H Clubs met at the national 4-H headquarters in Chevy Chase, Maryland. This was the first time that a Native American group had been hosted at the national 4-H headquarters. Whereas most of Florida is being developed for housing communities, the Seminole Tribe is able to recognize their strong heritage in agriculture and animal husbandry and the role it plays in their past and future.

169

ST. JOHNS COUNTY
BY: MARGO C. POPE

Forestry training school, 1961

St. Johns County 4-H has been developing future leaders for more than eighty-five years. Former county commissioners Earl Byrd, also a former national president of county commissioners, and Francis Brubaker served multiple terms on the commission, including terms as chairman. Their love of 4-H carried over into their adult years as they sponsored activities and helped when needed.

Another long-time 4-H member who has continued serving 4-H is sitting 7th Judicial Circuit Court Judge Clyde Wolfe. Local business leader Jim Browning, a former State 4-H Council president and also president of the 4-H Foundation, has given extensive leadership to the St. Johns Chamber of Commerce and the Economic Development Council.

The alumni of 4-H are found among the county's teachers and school administrators, law enforcement officers, business owners, farmers, religious leaders, funeral directors, military members, medical personnel, and government officials, both elected and long-time civil servants.

years sponsored the annual 4-H Camp at Crescent Beach and many 4-H service projects and group activities have been connected to beach conservation and enjoyment of water activities.

Brown's predecessor, Anna Heist, originated 4-H in the county and had 168 girls in ten clubs in 1922. Boys were the original members of the pig and corn clubs that eventually became co-educational. The county agent shared the 4-H duties with Miss Heist.

The county's 4-H history includes an all-female vegetable judging team that won state and national honors the first year women were eligible to participate in the 4-H vegetable judging competition. The county's male teams were consistent state and national winners as well. Likewise, Steve Simmons won state and national dairy judging events, enough to win him a spot on the U.S. team destined for international competition in London in 1950. Simmons later became a dairy farmer himself.

Adult leadership, too, earned recognition nationally when Foy Hartley, an adult leader during the 1950s, was recognized for her sewing accomplishments in a story in the national 4-H news.

In 1962, William Lockhart was named the National Citizenship Winner.

In the 1970s, county 4-H won the national Horticulture Beautification Award for the historical landscaping category.

Clubs have come and gone, changing with the need. The Hastings Community/School 4-H Club, founded by Miss Heist, ran from 1922 to the 1980s. Another long-time club was the Moultrie Community

But in 1922, 4-H in St. Johns County did not have an auspicious beginning. Chicken and tomato, corn, and pig clubs were the draws back then.

Nettie Ruth Brown, county 4-H agent from 1960 to 1985, sums it up best: "The St. Johns County 4-H Program started in 1922 with a chicken and tomato club, while camping on the beach learning to make periwinkle soup and scrambled eggs with [soda] crackers."

The beach played a key role in county 4-H since 1922. The Rotary Club of St. Augustine for many

First place Women's Vegetable Judging team, 1964. They won first place at state level and second place at national level. From left to right are Susan Foster, Joann Kovolski, Charlene Friday, and Mickey Mickler.

4-H Club, which functioned from the mid-1920s through the 1980s. The Happy Homemakers 4-H Club ran from the 1950s through 2006 with a break of three to four years.

The twenty-two-year-old 4-H Goat Club/Project is today's longest-running club, under the leadership of Sharon TerKeurst. The Buds and Blossoms 4-H Club, formerly 4-H Junior Gardeners, has been active since the mid-1980s.

The 4-H members have always been a part of community events and projects beyond 4-H. Among those activities, they have served on the food line for the Timber Growers Fish Fry, made ditty bags for the military during the Vietnam War, landscaped the Garden Center, collected for March of Dimes during Tag Day, operated booths during Cracker Day, and served as ushers for many years during the summer runs of *Cross and Sword*, a play about St. Augustine's founding, through the 1980s. Community organizations have reciprocated over the years with major sponsorships of 4-H events including the annual Fashion Revue, sponsored by the Pilot Club of St. Augustine, and the annual public speaking contest, sponsored by the Kiwanis Club of St. Augustine. The winners of these two activities have gone on to win in state competitions, too.

Today, twenty 4-H clubs/projects involve 240 youth who meet at least once a month, sometimes more often. More than 4,200 additional youth are in 4-H classroom enrichment programs. County 4-H activities include sewing, crafts, horse, goat, dog, poultry, shooting sports, GPS, public speaking, gardening, community service, and health (nutrition and fitness).

A tally of state leadership positions held by county 4-H youth, alumni, and leaders consists of two state Foundation presidents, five State Council presidents, and four State Council officers. Six 4-H alumni and adult leaders are in the state 4-H Hall of Fame.

Today's 4-H agent is Geralyn Sachs. Miss Brown is an advisor, in the state's 4-H Hall of Fame, and the 2006 recipient of the 4-H Lifetime Achievement Award.

St. Johns County 4-H Summer Camp, Camp Ocala, 2006

The 4-H Rocketry Project

ST. LUCIE COUNTY
BY: SUSAN MUNYAN

The 4-H club in St. Lucie County began in the late 1950s or early 1960s. Most of the clubs were girls' home economics clubs and boys were in livestock clubs. The oldest club that is still in existence is the Rocking Horse 4-H Club, which began in 1964.

As St. Lucie County went from being a primarily agricultural county to today's urban/rural mix, the 4-H clubs have developed in the same way. Mrs. Marguerite Brock served as 4-H agent until 1987. Susan Munyan then became 4-H agent and is still serving in this role.

In 1987, the 4-H population consisted of 112 4-H club members in approximately nine clubs. As of 2008, there are twenty-three clubs, with 300 members and over 30,000 4-H school enrichment members.

174

St. Lucie County Marine Science summer camp, 1980s. Seining.

St. Lucie County Gardening Program at Southern Oaks Middle School, 2004

St. Lucie County School Enrichment Program, embryology. Mrs. Babcock's first-grade class, 1990s.

In 1987, the 4-H projects were sewing, cooking, market swine, market steer, and horses. In 2008, additions to the program were made with projects such as environmental conservation, geology, marine science, art, photography, small animals, gardening, horticulture, public speaking, and skateboarding.

Events and activities that have been a part of St. Lucie County history are summer day camps. In the mid-1980s, the 4-H day camps centered on a marine science theme and took place twice during the summer. Currently, three weeks of day camps are provided which focus on discovering 4-H topics, entomology, and extreme sports.

The St. Lucie County Fair has been a major event since the 1960s. The 4-H club plays a big part in the fair events from market animals, horses, and small animals to skateboard demonstrations. In 2003, the St. Lucie County Fair moved to a new, bigger location on Midway Road in St. Lucie County.

The 4-H club in St. Lucie County continues to develop and reflect the changes that occur within the county. However, the 4-H grassroots of agriculture remain strong in 2008.

SUMTER COUNTY
BY: SARAH HENSLEY

Sumter County has deep roots in agriculture, from farming to large commercial dairy operations. The T. G. Lee family still owns property in Sumter County that local cattlemen lease for cow calf beef herds. The earliest history of 4-H in Sumter County is the first boys' corn club contest, held in Bushnell on November 16, 1915. At this time, the industry focused around livestock, vegetables, timber,

citrus, turpentine, tobacco, and cotton. The boys' clubs completed projects in these subject areas. The first agent in 1928 was I. R. Nolen, and in 1936, W. J. Platt. The first 4-H club was established in 1936. In 1941, Sumter County welcomed the first African-American agent to conduct programs for African-American youth: Mr. Alonzo Young. In the last ten years, Sumter County has initiated the

Civic engagement has always been important to the 4-H members of Sumter County, as you can see from this picture taken in the 1920s.

Sloan (Atkins) Farmer participates in the Hog 'n' Ham project at the University of Florida in the late 1990s.

Sumter County 4-H'ers participate in the one-hundred-year celebration of National 4-H. From front to back, left to right, are: Josh Stewart, Kristian Chancey, Tyler Foster, Mobley, Candy Munz, Lacey Wing, Samantha Daves, Jessica White, Kaycee Barco, Robin Foster, Erin Munz, Gloria Hayward, Gwen Mobly, Lisa Wing, Gerri Gatlin, Jay Mobley, Matt Wing, Michael Presley, Lauren Wood, Linda Burt, Mr. Wing, Danny Maddox, Martha Maddox, Mr. Mobley, Todd Stewart, and Candy Stewart. 2002.

The Poultry Bar-B-Q Contest at the Sumter County Fair provides youth with an opportunity to demonstrate food safety and preparation skills. Member Tony Lovett currently volunteers for the Sumter County 4-H Program.

Tropicana Public Speaking Contest and has had an increase in dairy exhibitors.

Project interests have diversified somewhat from the early days; however, in the rural county of Sumter, livestock and home economics projects have the highest enrollment. The fastest-growing project in Sumter County in 2007 was the 4-H dog project. Other projects are beef, swine, horse, sewing, goat, dairy, leadership, recreation, and arts and crafts. The 4-H camp has always been popular. Youth started camping at Camp McQuarrie and now attend Camp Ocala.

Current enrollment is approximately 180 youth. The longest-running club is the South Sumter Livestock Club, which was established in 1960 and has been active for forty-eight years. Two other clubs that have been active for an extended period of time are Windsong Riders and Friends and Sumter Saddle Ups, each over twenty-five years old.

The 4-H club in Sumter County is a family affair and part of the rural way of life that residents enjoy as

177

a part of daily living. Many former 4-H members are still volunteers and active in 4-H programming and in the Sumter County Fair. An example of the tradition of 4-H is a member of the Kountry Kids Dairy Club, Jamie (McClure) Graham, currently of Webster. Jamie participated in the 1977 State 4-H Dairy Show. Jamie later became the leader of Kountry Kids Dairy Club, where her daughters Jessica and Janet were active members who also participated in the State 4-H Dairy Show in the 1990s. Jamie is currently a member of the

Sumter County 4-H Advisory Committee and her daughters still assist with the local dairy judging contest. This is just one example of the many families who have been and who remain active in the county 4-H program, giving selflessly of their time, knowledge, and experiences.

The 4-H program in Sumter County has helped produce many fine young people and the number of former 4-H'ers residing and leading in Sumter County are a credit to the fact that 4-H truly does "make a difference."

SUWANNEE COUNTY
BY: KATHERINE ALLEN

Watermelon-cutting at Suwannee-Columbia Camp. Suwannee Springs, 1921.

The winners of the 1950 Florida State 4-H Club Tractor Driving Contest were, from left to right: Buford Butts, Suwannee County, first place; Homer Stewart, Escambia County, second place; and Errol Fielding, Columbia County, third place. The contest was held in conjunction with the 4-H short course at the University of Florida, Gainesville.

The 4-H club was started in Suwannee County by Agent J. A. Johnson in 1914. Boys' 4-H club work has the privilege of claiming to be the "oldest in the state," because Extension work was inaugurated first in Suwannee County when accepted by the State of Florida. The girls' 4-H tomato clubs were started in 1912 by the first county home demonstration agent, Mrs. Quarterman.

Suwannee County currently has an active and successful 4-H program that includes traditional activities from livestock judging and embryology to innovative interests focusing on robotics and bats. There are about ten clubs that include homeschoolers and range in subject matter, including a sharpshooter club and a horse club.

There is active participation in county events, Congress, Legislature, and residential camping. Residents of Suwannee County take pride in the local 4-H program and Extension receives outstanding support as a result. Some of the best volunteers and parents in the state help to make the best of Suwannee County even better.

TAYLOR COUNTY
BY: DIANE V. WHITFIELD

Taylor County 4-H history is written in the character and leadership achievements of generations of local families. Anabelle Peadon introduced 4-H to Mary Lou (Malone) Whitfield, age ninety-five, and Sarah Helen (Hendry) Steen, age ninety-three. They were young teens in 1925, when Miss Peadon encouraged them to start 4-H gardens. They planted, weeded, hoed, and kept records on their work. Doris (Agner) Lewis, eighty-four (and the best-known 4-H leader in Taylor County), remembers that she couldn't wait to join her older siblings in 4-H. She "watched with interest as my sister cared for her tomato plants as a Tomato Club member—a forerunner of the 4-H Club." When Floy Moses (LaValle), became home demonstration agent from 1926 to 1939, she organized the first local 4-H camp at Keaton Beach. R. S. Dennis was the county agent from 1926 to 1938.

180

In the 1940s, community schools in Shady Grove, Cabbage Grove, Fenholloway, Spring Warrior, Salem, Stephensville (Steinhatchee), and Perry Elementary offered 4-H meetings during the school day so rural children could use bus transportation. Mrs. Lyndall (Duckworth) Ellison remembers joining 4-H at Perry Elementary School in the 1940s. The 4-H projects for girls were primarily cooking and sewing. County Agent Dan McCloud (1938–1951) met with the boys and Home Demonstration Agent Ruth McKeown Elkins (1939–1953) worked with the girls, driving to the schools once a month. They made home visits to inspect crops, animals, and project work, and to share helpful information with families.

Taylor County Home Demonstration Agent Ethel (Paschal) Thompson and Janice (Jackson) Tedder prepare for a County Council meeting. (Photo courtesy Janice Tedder, 1960)

Taylor County's first community garden was planned and managed by 4-H member Anthony Flowers, with leadership and technical assistance (tractor work) provided by volunteer leader Earle Williams. This project won Anthony a trip to National 4-H Congress in Chicago, Illinois. (Photo courtesy Henry Davis collection, 1980)

Shady Grove School Principal Doris Lewis and Taylor County Agent Steiner Kierce (1951–1954) planned an award-winning beekeeping project, placing hives around the Shady Grove community.

Mr. Kierce and 4-H boys "robbed" the hives, and club members strained and sold the honey for project money. Mr. Kierce promoted 4-H by having the members interviewed on the radio. County Commissioner Malcolm Page remembers coming to town from Cabbage Grove, spending the night with relatives, talking on the radio, and getting back in time for school the next day. Ruth Milton (1953–1955) provided home demonstration and girls' 4-H leadership in Taylor County until accepting a position with the University of Florida. Morris Steen, the recently retired president of North Florida Community College, was a Shady Grove 4-H boy and joined collegiate 4-H at the University of Florida. He states, "I credit 4-H as much as anything in my life with helping me become who I am today."

Christine (Morgan) Goff, one of nine children, recalls how excited she, her siblings, and her friends were when they joined 4-H at their rural school during the '50s. She remembers learning to sew on a treadle machine and making and modeling a red crepe dress with matching purse. She was especially proud of winning trips to Camp Cherry Lake and to the 1956–1957 annual Florida State Girls' 4-H Club Short Course in Tallahassee. The week in Tallahassee "with meals prepared and indoor plumbing was very impressive for a country girl!"

Henry Davis became county agent in 1954 and had responsibility for the school 4-H clubs. Assistant County Agent Bill Smith (1959–1965) and Home Demonstration Agent Ethel (Paschal) Thompson (1958–1972) helped community and special interest clubs. The 4-H and Extension headquarters moved several times during these years but without disrupting youth activities. Dr. Selen (Lauterbach) Steen feels that "4-H helped train us to be successful adults," and her lifelong friend, Janice (Jackson) Tedder, agrees, saying, "4-H taught us to plan, practice, and persist with projects."

In 1963, Taylor County 4-H'ers were elected as presidents of both girls' and boys' State 4-H Councils, with Harriet Lewis (girls' state president) following in her mother's footsteps! The boys' state president was Clifford "Pete" Davis. Taylor County had twenty 4-H clubs during the 1960s, with 200 members led by thirty volunteers. Clubs were: Working H's, Chick-a-Dee, Green Acres, Tall Pines, Conservation Club, Go-Getters, Jolly Pals, and Helping Hands and Hearts. Neighborhood clubs were: Morgan Edwards, Shady Grove, Pisgah, Woods Creek, Johnson Stripling, Steinhatchee, Salem, and Foley. The Spring Warrior Club, established in 1959 by Lyndall Ellison and her family, was the first Taylor County 4-H club to be chartered; it remained active until 1990. Ellison children were among numerous state and national award-winners from this club. Assistant County Agent Jim Phillips and his wife Jan started the Tall Pines 4-H Club and made civic education, community service, and environmental awareness their focus. Robin (Gardiner) Poncia, educator and businesswoman, was a member of this club for seven years and provides this tribute to Jim Phillips: "We so loved and respected him. His knowledge and love of nature, his careful stewardship of the environment (long before it was popular) came together with his belief that we (the kids in the club) had something to offer this world."

In 1971, County Agent Henry Davis, Assistant County Agent Jim Phillips, and State Extension Forester Tony Jensen created the State 4-H Forest Ecology Program. Schools no longer host 4-H activities. Home Extension Agent Carol Mott (1972–1982) and Mr. Davis guided Taylor County 4-H as

181

programs integrated. In 1975, Leola Glenn was hired as program assistant. She helped 4-H'ers with their project work, from gathering information and making posters to practicing their presentations. As there were no African-American youth in 4-H when she was hired, Mrs. Glenn took on the task of increasing minority participation, going door-to-door for parental permission, providing transportation to meetings, and recruiting volunteer leaders. Atlanta attorney Michael Tedder remembers that "Henry Davis, Carol Mott, and Leola Glenn of the Taylor County Extension Office were like a second family to me...I hung around that County Extension office after school for many years."

The 1980s brought changes to the leadership of Taylor County 4-H. Mr. Davis retired in 1982 and Carol Mott left Perry. Realtor Ben Phillips stays in touch with Mr. Davis and considers him

Taylor County's first 4-H Steer Club. From left to right are: Georgia Davis, Pete Davis, Selen (Lauterbach) Steen, and Assistant County Agent Bill Smith, holding 4-H member Morris Steen's steer. (Photo courtesy Henry Davis collection, 1959)

"the most humble man—a role model to me." Clay Olson became county agent and Deborah Humphries was hired as home Extension agent. Mrs. Humphries brought the first environmental conservation information to Taylor County: a

recycling campaign. Her sons were active in county, district, and state 4-H; the youngest met his bride at Camp Cherry Lake! Another first occurred during the '80s. Three Bethea children from the Spring Warrior Club achieved State 4-H offices of treasurer and president: Andy, from 1981 to 1983; Clay, from 1983 to 1985; and Marilyn, from 1986 to 1988.

Taylor County sweeps State 4-H Council elections! The girls' and boys' State 4-H Council presidents were from Taylor County. From left to right are: Ethel Thompson, home economics agent; Harriette Lewis (Watts), Girls' State Council president; Pete Davis, Boys' State Council president; and Assistant County Agent Bill Smith. (Photo courtesy Doris Lewis collection, 1963)

In the 1990s, the Extension Office moved from the courthouse to a building with room for 4-H activities. An equine facility was built on the grounds. The Renegades 4-H Horse Club became one of the largest 4-H clubs in thirty years. Carol Sue and Jerry Register, with the help of thirty-five volunteers, led over sixty members to participate in horse judging, Horse Bowl, community service, horse camp at Camp Timpoochee, public speaking, horse science demonstrations, and to compete in county, district, state, and regional events.

Increasing demands on home Extension and a growing 4-H membership led citizens to successfully petition Taylor County government to add a 4-H agent position to the County Extension Program. Amy McMullen was the first fully county-funded agent from 1991 to 1995, followed by Heather Folsom from 1995 to 1997. Florida A&M University added a program assistant position, which is capably filled by Mae Ella Ray, reaching school and community groups with food and nutrition information.

In 1997, Lori Wiggins was hired as 4-H agent. Leaders Sharon Hathcock and Diane Whitfield were named State Volunteers of the Year. Home-school families discovered 4-H, and volunteer Cheryl Massey helped form the first clubs for homeschoolers. Members have been active, participating in 4-H Congress and Legislature. Home-school student Will Oberschlake served

as state treasurer and speaker of the house, and brother Ed was president of the senate. Agent Wiggins assisted Taylor, Suwannee, and Columbia counties in forming the state's first multi-county 4-H Horse Show Circuit; for over six years, the Tri-County Circuit has shared management, award banquets, and volunteers. Agent Wiggins has developed a unique 4-H Summer Day Camp Program. Five hundred youth each summer take part in week-long enrichment experiences, traveling to educational sites throughout north central Florida and participating in creative activities at the 4-H center. Senior and graduate 4-H'ers are trained and hired to staff the camps. Taylor County 4-H reaches over 6,000 students with the Tropicana Public Speaking competition in grades three through eight. Each spring, in collaboration with Ag in the Classroom, 4-H hosts 300 fifth-grade students, giving them a chance to see Florida farm animals and products up-close and personal.

UNION COUNTY
BY: COLAN L. COODY

As I asked other 4-H'ers over sixty years of age about 4-H history in Union County, I got some amazing tales. Now to preface this article, I must tell you that as a fairy tale starts out, "Once upon a time," a story from Union County starts out, "Man, you ain't gonna believe this…"

Working from my memory, and that has its own challenges, Union County 4-H was the place to be in the mid- to late 1920s. Boys wore those funny hats with the pointed corner and no bill. The girls were prim and proper in dresses and bonnets. According to the 4-H records of 1929, they sold cookies for a nickel at the courthouse to have

money to go to Camp Cherry Lake. They also took a bushel of squash and corn to eat while at the camp.

Many stories are told about Camp Cherry Lake, but no one can remember a name, or maybe they are trying to protect the people in the story. I vote for the latter, as many a story is told, but I just can't remember who it was. Like the day someone tall enough to reach the dinner bell put a "dirt dobber" nest inside, so when boys from another county rang the bell, the dirt dobbers would get on them.

The November 1927 4-H records convey this account of the 4-H fair held at Lake Butler School:

Canning class at the Union County Fair

The speaking by Congressman Greene and L. M. Rhodes were well attended and greatly appreciated. Probably if we were to look the State over, we would not find two more outstanding public men to speak on such an occasion than these two. Mr. Greene spoke in very high praise of Mr. Rhodes as being the man who is doing more for the up-building of agriculture in the state than anyone else. We are grateful to these gentlemen for lending us their services for one day and bringing us such fine messages.

In the 1929 records, Hugh Dukes won the Banker's Scholarship to the University of Florida, worth $250, for showing the best gilt in the state at the Pig Club Show in Jacksonville on November 20, 1929. This scholarship was given by Frank E. Dennis, National Stock Yards, Jacksonville, Florida.

In November 1930, cash premiums were given by County Board of Commissioners, Union County (It was never paid due to lack of funds during the Depression). The total of these awards was $41.50. This was a disappointment to the 4-H'ers, but almost everyone knew times were hard, and they understood.

Some of these outstanding 4-H'ers grew up and went off to fight in World War II. This was a difficult time in Union County. Money was tight. As the young men answered the call of their nation, the farming workforce became depleted. After the war, they gathered around Spires IGA, the main grocery store, and shared experiences, which have never been told to anyone who was not in the war. All that is ever said is, "We did what we had to do, and boy I am sure glad to see you." This is the answer my dad and uncles gave me as a boy in North Madison County.

Looking at the roll call of October 1, 1940, I see men and women that I have worked for and with as a youth in Union County. Mr. Page McGill will show you how to stack hay, his way. Mr. Billy McGill was one of my school principals, track coach at Lake City Community College, and founding and current member of the Union County 4-H Foundation, Inc. Mr. George Hayes was the past grand master of the Grand Masonic Lodge of the State of Florida, and a personal friend and advisor. Mr. Bryan Hendricks' son Steven and I graduated together. His daughter Linda was the principal of Lake Butler Elementary School for many years and a member of the Union County 4-H Foundation, Inc. His son Joe was a county commissioner. All of Bryan Hendricks's children were members of the Union County 4-H Program. Mr. Wilford Croft served as county commissioner and Union County property appraiser from 1960 until he retired in 1992. Mr. Croft also provided me the opportunity to pick tobacco. Now that's a real treat!

Other former 4-H'ers of Union County that have always provided support throughout the years include Mr. Melaine "Red" Clyatt, Union County commissioner; Mr. Canova Howard, owner of Ho-Bo Tractor Company (Yes, this is still John Deere country); Mr. Ricky Jenkins, Union County commissioner; and Mrs. Marjorie Driggers, historian for Union County (the Union County Museum is named after her). Mr. Glenn Howard

John Green Sapp and his 4-H project with 4-H Agent John Halloway

The 4-H and FFA Group with calves, 1953

was then, and is now, the best storyteller in the county.

As I started this article, I told you "as listened to." That is because the older 4-H'ers always say, "You are younger and let me tell you before I forget."

VOLUSIA COUNTY
BY: SHIRLEY ELLISON

The Volusia County 4-H Program dates back to 1914. At that time, the boys had the Corn Club and the girls had the Tomato Club, and the program was operated through the schools. The home demonstration agent visited rural schools to expand the program.

Mrs. Julia was the first home demonstration agent and the assistant was Susan Russell. The Extension Office was located in the basement of the DeLand Courthouse. Mr. T. R. Townsend was the first County Extension director.

The major programs at that time were short courses for boys and girls. Later, other short courses such as swine, forestry, safety, wildlife conservation, and farm animals were added for boys. The girls also wanted more choices, and so sewing, food and nutrition, food preservation, and home improvement all became part of the program.

Presently, the Volusia County 4-H Program includes Fashion Revue, the Share-the-Fun Talent Show, county events, Tropicana Public Speaking, judging teams, animal science, the 4-H County Council, community service, and involvement in the Volusia County Fair, Central Florida Fair, and Florida State Fair. There are over thirty clubs in the county participating in 4-H projects. Individual projects are integral to youth development and are encouraged. The many workshops we offer to 4-H'ers and the schools stress citizenship, leadership, and life skills. Volusia County is proud to be a part of District VIII. The counties of District VIII work very closely to plan activities such as summer camp at Camp Ocala, Junior Congress, the Area D Horse Show, Senior Retreat Community Service, and competitions in the Central Florida

Safety Demonstration, 1960s

Fair. Volusia County 4-H also works hard to prepare youth for Congress, Legislature, and other state events.

The longest-running club in Volusia County is the Glenwood Trailblazers of DeLeon Springs. This club has been in existence for thirty-seven years. The leader's name is Mrs. Karen Russi, and most of the parents of the youth are volunteers in the club. Their projects include bicycling, sewing, photography, Consumer Choices, and woodworking. The Trailblazers have strong ties to DeLeon Springs State Park. Largely due to their commitment and effort, this historical park was taken over by the State of Florida. They continue to participate in clean-ups, maintain the butterfly garden, and volunteer during special events such as their Community Pride project.

186

Joan Stewart, assistant home demonstration agent, and Larry Loadholtz, assistant county farm agent

Enrollment in Volusia County 4-H has steadily increased over the years. We attribute the growth to the introduction of programs into public and private schools, the involvement of homeschool groups, promotion of the program to community organizations and churches, and publicity. One of the most important school enrichment programs is Tropicana Public Speaking. Volusia County started the program in the 1990s and continues to work with fourth-, fifth-, and sixth-grade teachers in an effort to interest more youth in 4-H and what it has to offer. The 4-H Common Courtesy Academy, begun in 2004, is another important program that is offered to the community. Youth are taught etiquette, manners, and appropriate behavior.

There are many distinguished 4-H alumni from Volusia County: Mr. Larry Loadholtz of Seville, a 4-H'er who went on to become a 4-H agent and later the County Extension director; Alzada Fowler of Lake Helen, a member in the 1940s, who used her 4-H skills to become an elementary school teacher; Doris McWilliams of DeLeon Springs, now retired from early childhood education, who was a 4-H'er under the leadership of Ida Pemberton, the home demonstration agent at that time; Rhonda Richardson, the daughter of 4-H Program Assistant Shirley Ellison, who used the leadership skills she learned in 4-H to become a major in the United States Air Force; and Eric Meikle, who applied what he learned from community service by becoming a doctor of optometry.

The 4-H Girls' Poultry Show, 1936, sponsored by Sears Roebuck and Company

In 1927, at the fourth annual Volusia County Fair and Citrus Fruit Exposition, the home demonstration girls' clubs could enter canned and preserved foods as well as sewing samples of clothing and linens. Premiums ranged from $1.50 to $10.

At the third annual Volusia County Fair in March of 1956, community exhibits showcased 4-H clubs and 4-H'ers showed in the Beef Cattle

Show. From the 1940s to the 1960s, there was segregation in Volusia County, but there were 4-H clubs for African-American youth and these club members showed in the Volusia County Fair.

During the 1970s, major changes occurred in the local program. Community clubs became more prevalent and projects, such as photography, small engines, consumer education, and environmental education, expanded to address urban and suburban youth.

Today, the 4-H community clubs are still the heart of our program. In the past ten years, we have sent livestock judging teams, wildlife habitat evaluation teams, Horse Bowl teams, and hippology teams to several national competitions, and a horticulture judging team to national competition. In 2007, our junior and intermediate air rifle teams both won first place in the State Air Rifle Contest. Volusia County still values the 4-H Youth Development Program.

Volusia County 4-H'ers participate in a local parade.

The County Council issues a Proclamation each year during National 4-H Week that recognizes the contributions of 4-H. In January of 2008, Melanie Baggs, leader of the Ranch Raiders 4-H Club, was selected as the Southern Region Volunteer of the Year for the 2008 National 4-H Salute to Excellence Awards Program.

As we move into the next decade, Volusia County 4-H always stands ready and eager to meet the needs of the youth and community it serves. Even though the programs offered change, the basic principles remain the same: developing mature and responsible young people who will become the consumers and leaders of tomorrow. Volusia County has a diverse population and 4-H values the ethnicity, cultures, and needs of our community.

Volusia County 4-H sincerely appreciates all of the volunteers, leaders, youth, and staff over the last one hundred years that have devoted and committed themselves to the program and have given of their talents, time, and means to "make the best better."

WAKULLA COUNTY
BY: PRISCILLA WEAVER

In the early 1900s, to the best of our knowledge, W. T. Green was Wakulla County's first Extension agent as well as the founder of the first 4-H club, known as the Corn Club Boys. Wakulla County catered to the needs of agriculture for many years and later expanded into other areas to meet the needs of the community. Some of the projects offered through our area school were gardening, canning, sewing, animal husbandry, and field crops. Some of the clubs from the past are as follows:

- Corn Club Boys – W. T. Green
- The Crawfordville Club
- Wakulla's Best – Ed Swain and Sherry Fletcher
- Swifty Stitchers – Sue Ellen Strickland
- Crafty Carvers – Bea Kinyon and Diane Hayes
- Lucky Fours – Cynthia Gowdy
- Future Leaders – Elvira Williams
- The Go Getters – Ruby Allen and Betty Green
- County Liners – Cynthia Smith
- Leprechauns – Betty Morris
- The What Nots – Joe Thompson (deceased)

- The Sopchoppy 4-H Club – Cookie Coyle, Cordilla Porter, and Beverly Jefferson
- Good Ground Gardeners – Karen Tolley
- The Horticulture Club – Anita Brown
- Ambassadors Club – Anita Brown
- The Earth Club – Cathy Frank
- The Sprouts – Donna Howett
- Melody Makers – Shawna Weaver Aries
- Sea Searchers – Linda Hutton
- Home-school 4-H Club
- Mega Bytes, home-school computer club – Darlene Mills
- Knotty Needles, home-school sewing club – Ann Thurmond

As far back as 1938, Wakulla County had 4-H members camp at Cherry Lake. Mrs. Marjorie Sanders Gray, a member of Mrs. Penuel's 4-H club, remembers that when she was fifteen, her parents bartered for her camp fee with vegetables! She recalls one of the camp activities was making buttons using palmetto stems. There is no doubt that 4-H is still a fond memory for Mrs. Gray.

One 4-H alumnus, Henry Vause, recalled memories from the mid-'50s. The Crawfordville Club met in the back of the former Crawfordville High School. Their project area was animal science. He had poultry and other members had swine and cattle. They all came from farm families. Mr. Vause recalled that his trip to Tallahassee was on national TV in regards to their animal science project. This was a big event for the teen members in the late '50s. Mr. Vause said he would never forget the trip to 4-H Camp Cherry Lake. Surprisingly, even though the teens lived on the Gulf Coast, they could not swim. Mr. Vause said that they arrived at camp on Monday and by Friday they could all swim. He highly commends 4-H for its positive effect on youth. Mr. Vause graduated from Wakulla High School in 1960 and went on to become a carpentry teacher. Mr. Vause was also a county commissioner.

As community needs changed, so did 4-H. From corn clubs to computers, the county now has an abundance of resources available to the 4-H program and volunteer leaders through the University of Florida and the USDA. In keeping with tradition, the program continues to meet the needs and interest of youth with the following clubs:

- Kapra Kids, dairy goat club – Priscilla Weaver
- Arts-n-Crafters, craft club – Wanda Murray
- Target Smashers, shooting sports club – Mark Murray
- Horsemasters, horse club – Tracie Churchard
- Teen Leaders, leadership club – Angie Bradshaw
- Pony Pals, cloverbud horse club – Lori Westbrook
- School 4-H Club – Mrs. Bartnick's class, which included Marine Explores, Healthy Kids, and 4-H Peeps Club
- School 4-H Club Wild Adventures – Mrs. Callaghan's class

- School 4-H Club Fire Flys – Mrs. Mohr's class
- Sea Serpents 4-H Club – Angie Bradshaw and Scott Jackson

Kapra Kids, the 4-H dairy goat club, is the longest-running club in Wakulla County. The first meeting was held in September of 1985 with twelve members. Through the years, the club has had as many as fifteen and as few as eight members enrolled. This is a specialty club and the majority of the projects have been in the area of raising and managing healthy and profitable dairy goats. This involves accurate recordkeeping, animal science,

Wakulla County Events, Share-the-Fun, 1987. From left to right are Nina Brown, Susie Gilbert, Shawna Weaver, Anita Rozier, and Amy Reed.

judging, showing, safe milking practices, and the importance of a healthy product entering the food chain. Kapra Kids has actively participated in the following community service projects: food drives, Easter egg hunts, working with the elderly, Wakulla County beach clean-up, summer camps, and drug awareness workshops. The Kapra Kids 4-H Club is led by Ken and Priscilla Weaver, and they can boast that their children and grandchildren all participated in this club.

There are three individuals who have been instrumental within Wakulla County 4-H programs:

Vera Harvey, Dale Bennett, and Cathy Frank. These three individuals have all served various leadership roles with summer camps, school enrichment programs, 4-H clubs, and special interest projects. Due to the dedication of County Extension Director Dale Bennett, the county now has a new and modern Extension facility for 4-H and the community.

The most recent distinguished alumni of Wakulla County 4-H is Jim Tart. Jim was a grand champion exhibitor in the annual Swine Show for many years. He is also a part of the 2006 University of Florida national champion football team.

Target Smashers 4-H Club with Dale Bennet (founder), an agent for twenty-two years

WALTON COUNTY
BY: LAURA BOWDEN

The Walton County 4-H Program was the main entertainment and pastime in the Bowden family. The different project areas that were available gave everyone in the family something to do. Some of the children were into animals and some were into Share-the-Fun. Times and faces changed, but the 4-H program is still here for youth of Walton County and caring volunteers are ready to teach life skills by way of interesting programs and outings. Now, twenty years later, Laura Bowden sees the same youth that she drove around or chaperoned, and encouraged to take steps to try new things, becoming volunteers themselves. They have told her that the best memories they have as a youth are when they participated in 4-H events. The youth knew that they were safe and could have fun. The 4-H club is here for youth and is an exceptional youth program where youth can take the skills they learn and use them in their adult lives.

Clogging is a popular act for Share-the-Fun contests.

Walton County 4-H'ers, 1994

WASHINGTON COUNTY
BY: WASHINGTON COUNTY EXTENSION

Washington County 4-H began in the early 1920s and focused on livestock and home economics projects. When camping began at Camp Timpoochee, participants were transported to camp by boat. The fee for attending camp was food items, such as chickens or vegetables grown in the youth's gardens.

The Livestock Club in Washington County has been running for thirty-three years. Youth participate in dairy, steer, and swine projects. This club has been led by several families throughout its existence: the Solger family, Pate family, Webb family, Norton family, and Savelle family.

Leaders of Florida Boys' 4-H Club Council, 1949–1950. From left to right: Ralph Carter, Chipley, reporter; Jack Parker, Paisley, treasurer; Charles Allison, Umatilla, secretary; Lawrence Shackleford, Wauchula, vice-president; and Dennis Ray, DeFuniak Springs, president.

As competition has always had a place in 4-H project work, Washington County is proud of many participants. In 1983, George Fisher won first place at the State 4-H Automotive Driving Contest and a trip to the national contest. In 2000, the Washington County 4-H Livestock Judging Team won first place at the state contest and traveled to nationals. In 2008, 4-H Shure Shots—Brandon Porter, Jamey Hayes, and Cooper Holmes—won first place in the senior division at a state shooting sports contest. Major programs that are currently practiced in Washington County are shooting sports, robotics, livestock, and environmental sciences.

FLORIDA 4-H
Club Foundation, Inc., and Hall of Fame

The late 1950s and early 1960s were times of dynamic change for the 4-H program. Programs were expanding; volunteers were assuming greater roles and private dollars were being accepted. The need for a foundation was clear to 4-H staff.

On January 30, 1963, after seven years of commitment, planning, and action, the dream of the Florida 4-H Club Foundation became a reality. Charter members were M. O. Watkins, Joe N. Busby, Emily King, Anna Mae Sikes, Ann E. Thompson, Woodrow W. Brown, Elosie Johnson, Grant M. Godwin, and F. S. Perry. The 4-H Foundation raised a little over $500 in outside support that founding year. Today, it raises millions and has been lauded as "a masterpiece of foresight" (Woeste, Dr. John).

Just as importantly, during the first few years of the Foundation's existence, critical achievements and procedural tests occurred. Board membership began to include business and industry leaders. Legal status for the camp operations was clarified. Fundraising policies were established.

The 4-H Foundation is a tax-exempt nonprofit educational foundation approved under section 501(c)3 of the Internal Revenue 170(b)(1) Code. A volunteer board of directors elected from among 4-H friends, donors, and Extension representatives governs the Foundation. The headquarters are at the University of Florida in Gainesville.

194

The purposes of the Florida 4-H Foundation are to support the mission of the 4-H Youth Development Program, promote 4-H to additional potential partners, and provide stewardship in resource management.

Highlights of the past forty-six years include:

- 4-H membership has grown from 46,500 to over 234,000;

- The number of volunteers has increased from 3,500 to nearly 11,000;

- Annual funds have grown from $20,000 to over $200,000;

- The number of donors has increased from 30 to over 2,500;

- Camp operating funds have increased from $38,000 to nearly $1 million per year; and

- Management of endowed gifts have totaled nearly $3,000,000.

The Florida 4-H Foundation is a testament to people of vision. Their unwavering commitment to Florida's youth has helped millions to develop and mature into tomorrow's citizens.

FLORIDA 4-H
HALL OF FAME

The Florida 4-H Hall of Fame was created in 2002 during the National 4-H Centennial to recognize and celebrate those people who have made a significant impact on 4-H. This award honors volunteers, supporters, staff, and pioneers who made major contributions to 4-H at a local and state level.

INDUCTEES

2002

Helen Adler
B. J. Allen
Joe and Leslie Allen
Diane Anderson
Dr. Robert A. Anderson
A. T. Andrews
Rance A. Andrews
Walter B. Arnold, Jr. *
Fred W. Barber *
Doris Base *
Wilmer Bassett *
Dr. M. Langley Bell
Arthur Bissett
Raymond W. Blacklock *
James J. Brasher *
Honorable F. Allen Boyd
Floy Britt *
Nettie Ruth Brown
Reginald L. Brown
Woodrow W. Brown *
James E. Browning
Sandra Brubaker *
Joe N. Busby
Earl Byrd
Lamar Camp
Benjamin Campen
Isaac Chandler, Jr.
Maxine Clayton
Doyle Conner
Louise Cox
James A. Croft
Jacqueline DuPont
Virgil L. Elkins *
Barbara Eveland *
Susanne G. Fisher

Helen H. Fleming
Lester C. "Terry" Floyd *
E. Darwin Fuchs
P. Steven Futch
Louis Gilbreath
Francis Gindl
Betty Lou Glassburn
James Glisson
Carol Ann Gollnick
James E. Gorman *
Honorable Bob Graham
Thomas and Earlece Greenawalt
Hariot Greene
Willie Haas
Nadine Hackler
Marie Hammer
C. M. Hampson *
Aubrey "Luther" Harrell *
Mary N. Harrison
Oscar Harrison
Lisa T. Hinton
Kevin E. Hyde
Anthony S. "Tony" Jensen *
Audrey B. Johnson
Louise R. Johnson
Bette R. Jones
Deloris Mae Jones
Lester W. Kalch
Judy A. Keller
Emily E. King
Robert E. King
Donald W. Lander
Louis E. Larson, Jr.
Mary L. C. Leon
R. Earle Lucas, Jr.
D. R. "Billy" Matthews *

John and Mary McKeown
Kenneth S. McMullen *
Norman R. Mehrhof *
Damon Miller, Sr.
Ruth L. Milton
Judson Minear
Herbert F. "Herb" Morgan
Honorable Bill Nelson
Dan and Sara Nicholson
Marie Nickels *
James and Linda Parks
Rayburn "Kent" Price
Honorable Adam Putnam
Phoebe Hodges Raulerson
Clarence W. Reaves *
Nancy Alward Roberts
Warren E. Schmidt
Marylou W. Shirar
Thomas C. Skinner *
James M. Stephens
Lorene Stevens *
Alice Storms
Henry F. Swanson
Wendell H. Taylor
Walter G. Thomas
David W. Timberlake
Wilma Tindell *
James N. Watson
John T. Woeste

2003

Linda Cook
Nell Ohff
Paul Dinkins
Shirley Bond

2004

Max Hammond
Melinda Penny Gamot
Joy Wren Satcher
Joan Hughes Odom

2005

Mary Faith Urquhart
Bernard H. Clark
Sandy Shaw Bekemeyer

2006

Earl Ray Gill
Marjorie Modesky
H. Fred Dietrich III
Gladys Freeman
Frank Sullivan

2007

E. T. York
Marilyn Halusky
Robert Renner
Gene and Cordella LaRoe

2008

Larry B. Williams
Sue Young Bledsoe
Sandra J. Blackadar
Fred and Linda Burnett

*Posthumous honoree

195

BIBLIOGRAPHY

"A Brief History of Florida: From the Stone Age to the Space Age." *My Florida: Cultural, Historical, and Information Programs.* [Online] Available at http://dhr.dos.state.fl.us/facts/history/summary

Aalberg, R. *The Manatee County Extension Service: 80 years of service (1918–1998).* Palmetto, FL: Manatee County Extension Service, November 1998.

Brevard County Home Demonstration Club. Scrapbook, 1938–1939. Cocoa, FL: Brevard County Cooperative Extension Service Archives at Brevard County Agricultural Center.

Butler, Lynnie. Personal scrapbook (personal photographs with captions, newspaper articles without name of newspaper or dates). Records: 1934–2008.

Campbell, Anne J. *DeSoto County News.* Arcadia, FL: DeSoto County News, March 17, 1918.

Cordell, A. Extension Horticulturist II. "*Camp Co Ho De*," *A 4-H Retreat on the Beach.* 2006.

Cloutier, M. M. "Shiny Shots." *Palm Beach Daily News*, Archives, 1925.
    [Online] Available at http://shinyshots.palmbeachdailynews.com/pages/photo_page.php?mm=1481896&gallery

Cooper, J. Francis, ed. *Dimensions In History.* Tallahassee, FL: Rose Printing Company, Inc., 1976.

County Agriculture Agents. *Annual Narrative Report.* 1947, 1954, 1958.

County Record, The, February 20, 2008, p. 3.

County Record, The, October 9, 1975, p. 6.

Dymond, R. "4-H land judging team wins state title." *Bradenton Herald* (March 30, 2004), p. C8.

Everglades Research and Education Center (EREC). University of Florida. [Online] Available at http://erec.ifas.ufl.edu/erechistory.htm

Extension Staff. Santa Rosa County Extension 75th Anniversary, 1989.

Fazio, Gail (Ball). Brevard County 4-H Horse Program alumna. Telephone interview, January 2008.

Florida 4-H Program Handbook, The

Florida 4-H Website. [Online] Available at http://www.florida4h.org

Florida Memory Project Website, The. [Online] Available at http://www.floridamemory.com

Florida State University Archives

Greenawalt, T. Glow. *Little Glowworm.* Palmetto, FL: Manatee 4-H, p. 1.

Halsten, Rowena and Pat Alazracki. *Brevard County Extension Homemakers Council History 1934–1973.* p. 1

Harper, J. *4-H Pizza Garden: An Agricultural Adventure.* SP AGL 20, University of Florida IFAS.

Hillsborough County Home Demonstration Annual Club Scrapbooks: 1930, 1938–1939, 1940–1941, 1945–1946.

Hink, Jean M. Observed the floor in Clayton Hall, Pasco County Fairgrounds. Dade City, FL: February 2008.

Hoadley, Tom. "History of the Palm Beach Courthouse." [Online] Available at http://www.palmbeachbar.org/members/Crthse_History.pdf

Holland, Mary Ketus Deen. *Unto This Land: A History of the St. Johns Park Area of Flagler County and the Pioneer Settlers and their Descendants.* 2007. p. 71–73. Institute of Food and Agricultural Sciences website. [Online] Available at http://www.ifas.ufl.edu

Jasper News, The. Newspaper clippings. 1956–1971.

Jones, Evelyn. "The Girls' Side of the 4-H Story," *Annual Report.* Florida Agricultural Extension Service. Institute of Food and Agricultural Sciences. University of Florida. 1960. p. 37.

Kersey, A. Florida Association of Extension 4-H Agent. *Annual Report.* Polk County, downloaded from archives, January 14, 2008.

Lewis, M. D., et al. *The history and people of Hamilton County.* St. Petersburg, FL: Southern Heritage Press.

Lovelace, Mary C. Henry. *1967 National 4-H Report Form and Record Book*, Dade City, FL.

McKillop, Jeanne L. "Rough Draft of Duval County History."

Melton, Howard. *Foot Prints and Landmarks.* (Pine Level County Seat) & 30 (Early Schools), Arcadia, FL: Melton, 2002. p. 6.

Morris, Betty. "Memoirs of a Tomato Girl." *Florida Today* (May 5, 1989), Section D, p. 1.

National 4-H Headquarters Website. [Online] Available at http://www.national4-hheadquarters.gov

Nieland, L. T. "Agricultural Clubs Win Poultry Prizes." *Flagler Tribune* (February 23, 1928), p. 1.

———. County Agents Column. *Flagler Tribune* (October 21, 1928), p. 2.

———. "4-H Club Forestry Members to Make Trip on Saturday." *Flagler Tribune*, p. 2.

———. "Members 4-H Club Attend Volusia Fair." *Flagler Tribune* (May 2, 1929), p. 1.

O'Berry, J. "4-H changing with the times." Palmetto, FL: Manatee County Extension Service, May 1989, p. 1.

Pinellas County 4-H Youth Development. Pinellas County/University of Florida IFAS Extension Three-Year Strategic Plan, September 2006.

Polhill, Frank L. "Flagler County Booth at Fair." *Flagler Tribune* (November 18, 1954), p. 1.

————. "Flagler County 4-H Clubbers Return Home with Honors from Orlando Dairy Show." *Flagler Tribune* (February 25, 1960), p. 2.

————. "6th Annual Livestock and Poultry Show." *Flagler Tribune* (January 15, 1955), p. 1.

Ruskin Extension Homemakers Club. *The Shopper and Observer News* (1974).

Salazar, Carolyn. "Grahams Celebrate; Recall Dynasty's Birth." *The Miami Herald* (January 31, 2002), p. 3, NW.

Sanford Herald newspaper.

Seminole County 4-H Office Records.

State Archives of Florida. The Florida Department of State Website.

Storner, Don. "Looking to the Future: 4-H Opportunities."

Swanson, Henry F. *Countdown for Agriculture in Orange County Florida.* 1975.

Taylor, Nettie W. "Home Demonstration Agent's Report," 1935.

Tobias, B. 4-H Agent. Pinellas County YouthMapping, *Bridging Our Vision with Experience Report* (September 2001).

25th Annual Home Demonstration Short Course Jubilee (1912–1937), Manuscript Collection 91, Scrapbook. University Archives, Department of Special and Area Studies Collections, George A. Smathers Libraries, University of Florida, p. 30.

Watkins, M. O., "Seminole Indians on the Peace Path." *Dimensions in History.* J. Francis Cooper, ed. Gainesville, FL: Alpha Delta Chapter Epsilon Sigma Phi, 1976. p. 82–86.

Webster's New Dictionary and Thesaurus

Woeste, Dr. John. UF Professor Emeritus and former Director of the Florida Cooperative Extension Service. Personal interview, April 2008.

Yonge, P. K. "Library of Florida History." [Online] Available at http://www.uflib.ufl.edu/spec/pkyonge/index.html

ABOUT THE AUTHORS

JULIE SWIFT WILSON is a native Floridian, born and raised in Sarasota. At the age of nine, she joined 4-H in Sarasota County and was an active member for nine years. During her 4-H career, Julie held various club offices and participated in the swine, horse, and leadership projects each year. She started working in the Florida 4-H State Office as summer event staff in 2000. She also became a licensed Equine Sports Massage Therapist while attending Equissage in Round Hill, Virginia. Julie continues her employment with the University of Florida 4-H Youth Development Program as secretary for the Regional Specialized 4-H Agents. She says that 4-H has instilled many life lessons in her. She gained a lot of knowledge, many friendships, and a love for animals through the program as a youth participant and as an adult. Julie intends to stay involved with the 4-H program and may become a 4-H volunteer leader one day. Julie married her husband, Chuck, in 2005. They have one son, one horse, and two dogs.

LAURA C. LOK held the position of public relations coordinator for the 4-H Youth Development Program from March 2006 to April 2008. She is currently a marketing manager at Maupin House Publishing in Gainesville, Florida. With no previous 4-H experience, Laura enjoyed her time with the program because she was able to touch the lives of youth in a positive way through her marketing efforts. She says that telling the stories of these amazing youth and adults was a very fulfilling part of her job. She received her B.A. in Organizational Communications from the University of Tulsa. Laura married her husband, Benjamin, in 2005. They have two dogs and two cats.

Florida Farm Bureau

The Voice of Florida Agriculture

CONGRATULATIONS 4-H!

FROM FLORIDA FARM BUREAU

I am pleased to recognize the accomplishments of 4-H during its Century Year.

The history of the Florida 4-H Youth Development Program parallels that of the Florida Farm Bureau Federation, the state's general agricultural organization. Farm Bureau has long supported 4-H nationwide, and Florida is no exception.

Florida Farm Bureau has supported 4-H and other youth development programs and members of our staff and volunteer leaders have proudly served on the board of the Florida 4-H Foundation. Many of those leaders have themselves acquired leadership skills, a positive sense of self and the ability to participate in the world of work, beginning with their participation in 4-H programs as youths.

4-H continues to play a vital role in developing our youth. Congratulations on 100 years of accomplishment.

John Hoblick,
President

Hardee County 4-H Foundation

 Cracker Trail
Leaders: Monica Stevenson & Kay Crews

 Heart of Hardee
Leaders: Teresa Carver & Tracy Pate

 Country Clovers
Leaders: Joy & Robert Roberts,
Susan & Bobby Brewer

 Thundern' Hooves Horse Club
Leaders: Kim & Steve McVay

 Fort Green Community
Leaders: Charlotte Yake & Amy Brown

 River Rats Community Club
Leaders: Jacque & Danny Weeks

 Green Acres
Leaders: Joy Brummett & Sara Polk

 Hardee Hot Shots Shooting Sports Club
Leaders: Peggy & Lucas Chancey

 Hardee Beef & Bacon
Leaders: Roy & Wendy Petteway,
Tommy & Barbara Arnold

 The Castaways Sport Fishing
Leaders: Rex & Patricia Richey

 Moovers & Shakers Dairy Club
Leaders: Tami Hunt

507 Civic Center Drive
Wauchula, FL 33873-9460
Phone (863) 773-2164
Fax (863) 773-6861

Ms. Nettie Ruth Brown's 4-H experience began growing up in Baker County along with her seven brothers and sisters. They participated in 4-H activities and attended camp at Cherry Lake. After graduating from high school and college, Ms. Brown began her career in Tennessee. In 1960, after serving eight years as a home demonstration agent, she assumed the responsibilities for the home economics and girls' 4-H programs in St. Johns County, Florida. Ms. Brown served as the interim County Extension director for two years. In 1978, she became responsible for the St. Johns County 4-H Program. Ms. Brown held the position of 4-H coordinator until her retirement in 1985. During her career in Extension, Ms. Brown was very active in various professional organizations. In 1975, she served as president of the National Association of Extension Home Economists. In recognition of her outstanding career, Ms. Brown has been recognized with the NAEHE Distinguished Service Award, the National 4-H Agents Distinguished Service Award, the 4-H Legislative Life Time Achievement Award, the Florida 4-H Hall of Fame Award, the Enterprising Women of Florida Leadership Award, the Berry College Distinguished Service Award, and the Baker County High School Hall of Fame Award.

Ms. Brown always insisted on quality and she elevated the 4-H program to prominence and respect. With an energetic and creative leadership style, 4-H members earned many state and national awards in public speaking and horticultural demonstrations. Ms. Brown authored publications on 4-H speaking demonstrations, clothing, table setting, and food contests. Ms. Brown assisted with the organization and charter of the Florida Association of Extension 4-H Agents. She gave her assistance in the development of seminars and exhibits for the national meeting in Florida. Since her retirement, Ms. Brown remains an active supporter of Extension programs.

providing a **Fresh** start for **Florida** kids every day

Thank You Florida 4-H!

Florida Department of Agriculture and Consumer Services • Charles H. Bronson, Commissioner

 **Santa Fe
Soil and Water
Conservation District**

Serving Columbia County Since 1942

Front row: Don Stevens, Supervisor – Bernice Brickles, Secretary – Will Brown, Chairman – Rufus Ogden, Secretary/Treasurer – Al Oliver, NRCS District Conservation. Back row: Hugh Thomas, Environmental Specialist, Florida Department of Agriculture – Lamar Moseley, Vice Chairman – Don Spradley, Supervisor.

Santa Fe Soil and Water Conservation District in Columbia County, Florida, coordinated and hosted the Suwannee Regional Envirothon from 1993 till 2006. We donate coloring books and crayons to the kindergarten students at the beginning of the school year to go into tote bags that each student will receive as they start school. We had a student from the middle school win the state Poster Contest. We have a booth at the Columbia County Fair every year. We contribute to the 4-H Foundation and other educational programs.

Of course we're a supporter of Florida's 4-H program.
Have you seen how much these kids eat?

Winn-Dixie salutes Florida 4-H for its 100 years of serving the young people of Florida.

Getting better all the time.

Congratulations

Florida 4-H, as you

celebrate 100 years of

service in teaching young

people leadership,

citizenship and

life skills.

Florida Fruit & Vegetable Association
www.ffva.com
P.O. Box 948153
Maitland, FL 32751
321.214.5200

UF UNIVERSITY of FLORIDA
IFAS Extension
4-H Youth Development

THANKS!

To All Who Have Been a Part of 4-H and Made It What It Is Today!

From the State 4-H Office

The Florida Marlins
Community Foundation is a
Proud Supporter of
Florida 4-H!

*Together We Are Making
The Best Better.*

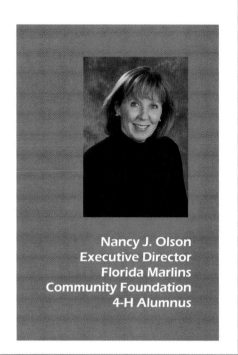

Nancy J. Olson
Executive Director
Florida Marlins
Community Foundation
4-H Alumnus

The Florida Association of Extension 4-H Agents (FAE4-HA) at a Glance

- 1969—Small group of 4-H agents start meeting informally to exchange program ideas.
- Ernie Cowen (Orange Co.) was the first agent to become fully aware of the National Association of 4-H Extension Agents (NAE4-HA) and its opportunities.
- November 1970—Cowen, Leah Hoopfer (Pinellas Co.) and Alice Kersey (Polk Co.) attend National 4-H Agents meeting at Perdue University.
- 1971—As state contact for Florida, Kersey attended a Southern Region ECOP meeting for presidents in Atlanta.
- July 1975—Richard Freeman, Southern Region Director, comes to present the NAE4-HA to Florida's 4-H Agents. He was prepared with information about how to organize a state association.
- Nettie Ruth Brown (St. Johns Co.) was nominated by B.J. Allen to chair the organizational meeting, where elections were held.
- First officers of FAE4-HA: John Smehyl (Hillsborough Co.) as President, Alice Kersey as secretary, and Bob Renner, Jr. (Marion Co.) as treasurer. Smehyl soon resigned from his position and Shirley Bond (Pinellas Co.) served as the first active president. Bond was elected to serve an additional term while FAE4-HA became a fully functional state association.
- Joy Satcher of Brevard County was designated our first member to receive the Distinguished Service Award
- An association annual meeting time was established. It would be held at Florida's State Extension Administrative Conference.
- An annual award was established to honor "the Extension employee who develops and has printed the best 4-H materials".
- FAE4-HA's bid to host the National Meeting in 1981 was successful. The 1981 meeting was held in Orlando.
- Mary Williams (Nassau Co.) served as NAE4-HA President in 2004-2005.
- In 2008, the FAE4-HA had a membership of 94 members and 19 lifetime members.
- FAE4-HA won the bid to host the 2012 National Association of Extension 4-H Agents Annual Meeting and Professional Development Conference to be held in Orlando, Florida.

FAE4-HA continues to provide leadership for the 4-H professionals in the state. The association was developed by strong-willed, determined and devoted individuals and continues to be lead by strong-willed, determined and devoted individuals.

POLK COUNTY 4-H FOUNDATION, Inc.
BARTOW, FL

The Polk County 4-H Foundation congratulates
Florida 4-H
for 100 years of Excellence in Youth Development!

2007-2008 OFFICERS & DIRECTORS

James A. Cook, Jr., President
Cheryl Fulford, Vice President
Georgiann Sumner, Secretary
Sylvia Fletcher, Treasurer
Kenneth B. Allen
David Byrd
Ginger Fortner
Colleen C. Holland
Heather Nedley
Delphine Pullar
Michele A. Purcell
Byron Walker
Ned Waters

**INVESTING IN POLK COUNTY'S YOUTH AND THE VOLUNTEERS
WHO TEACH AND LEAD THEM**

Ruth Milton was an active 4-H member in Marion County, participating in food, clothing, gardening, canning, and citizenship projects and activities. While she taught home economics she served as a volunteer 4-H leader. Milton became an Extension professional in 1952, serving as home demonstration agent in Gulf County. She later moved to Taylor County and then to Manatee County, where she became the assistant agent with primary responsibility for 4-H. During her tenure on the state 4-H staff, she served as liaison for the 4-H home economics projects. She produced and edited many of the 4-H publications, program guides, and manuals, including co-authorship of "4-H Develops Capable Citizens," a chapter in Dimensions In History. One of her greatest and lasting efforts, which received national acclaim, was the development of Florida 4-H Legislature and the Community Pride Program. These programs serve as a guide to developing stronger leadership, better citizenship, and interest in civic and community activities among participating 4-H members.

Ruth Milton
Associate Professor
Emeritus